POASIS
II

WESLEYAN POETRY

Also by Pierre Joris

Poetry

Interglacial Narrows (Contra Mundum Press, 2023)

Fox-trails, -tales & -trots: Poems & Proses (Luxembourg: Black Fountain Press, 2020)

The Book of U / Le livre des cormorans, with Nicole Peyrafitte (Luxembourg: Editions Simoncini, 2017)

Canto Diurno: Choix de poèmes 1972–2014 (Paris: Le castor astral, 2017)

An American Suite (Inpatient Press, 2016)

Gulf Od Vraku K Pohromé, Czech translation by Barbora Hrušková (Prague: Spolek přátel Psího vína, 2016)

Barzakh (Poems 2000–2012) (Black Widow Press, 2014)

Maquif: Poemas y ensayos, Spanish selected poems (La Otra, Mexico DF, 2014)

Meditations on the Stations of Mansur al-Hallaj (Chax Press, 2013)

The Gulf (Between You & Me) (The Crossing, 2013)

learn the shadow (unit4art, 2012)

Canto Diurno #4: The Tang Extending from the Blade, ebook (Ahadada Books, 2010)

Aljibar & Aljibar II (Editions PHI, 2007; 2008)

Routes not Roots, audio recording (CD Baby, 2007)

Meditations on the Stations of Mansur Al-Hallaj 1–20 (Chax Press, 2006)

The Rothenberg Variations (Wild Honey Press, 2004)

Fin de siècle-Phantombild; Ausgewählte Gedichte 1974–2000 (Editions PHI, 2004)

Permanent Diaspora (Duration Press, 2003)

Poasis: Selected Poems 1986–1999 (Wesleyan University Press, 2001)

h.j.r. (Otherwind Press, 1999)

out/takes (Backwoods Broadsides, 1999)

La dernière traversée de la manche (Editions PHI, 1995)

Winnetou Old (Meow Press, 1994)

Turbulence (St. Lazaire Press, 1991)

The Irritation Ditch (Parentheses Writing Series, 1991)

Janus (St. Lazaire Press, 1988)

Breccia: Selected Poems 1972–1986 (Editions PHI, 1987; Skylight Press, 2014)

Net/Work (Spanner Books, 1983)

The Book of Luap Nalec (Ta'wil Books, 1982)

make it up like say (1982)

Tracing (Arc Press, 1982)

The Broken Glass (Pig Press, 1980)

Old Dog High Q (Writers Forum, 1980)

Body Count (Twisted Wrist, 1979)

The Tassili Connection (Ta'wil Books, 1978)

Tanith Flies (Ta'wil Books, 1978)

Hearth-Work (Hatch Books, 1977)

Antlers I–XI (New London Pride, 1975)

A Single-minded Bestiary (poet & peasant press, 1974)

Trance/Mutations (1972)

The Fifth Season (Strange Faeces Press, 1971)

PIERRE JORIS POASIS II

SELECTED POEMS 2000–2024

Wesleyan University Press   MIDDLETOWN, CONNECTICUT

Wesleyan University Press
Middletown CT 06459
www.wesleyan.edu/wespress

© 2025 Estate of Pierre Joris
All rights reserved
Manufactured in the United States of America
Designed and composed in Centaur MT Pro
by Julie Allred, BW&A Books, Inc.

Lines quoted from Allen Mandelbaum's translation of Dante are from
Purgatorio: A Verse Translation (New York: Bantam Books, 1988).

Excerpt from score of "Rigwreck" by Gabriel Jackson © 2015 Oxford
University Press, used with permission. All rights reserved.

Published with the support of
Kultur|lx Arts Council Luxembourg

Library of Congress Cataloging-in-Publication Data
available at https://catalog.loc.gov/
paper   ISBN 978-0-8195-0195-0
ebook   ISBN 978-0-8195-0196-7

5 4 3 2 1

for Nicou,
comme toujours & avec sa rime

CONTENTS

Acknowledgments   xiii

from PERMANENT DIASPORA

"This afternoon Dante"	3
The word, the mawqif	4
Tuesday, May 23rd 2000	5
E.P.: heard, not seen	6
Writing / Reading #18	7
for Gerrit Lansing at 75	11

from THE ROTHENBERG VARIATIONS

Variation #1	15
Variation #2	16
Variation #3	17
Variation #6	18
Variation #9	19

from LEARN THE SHADOW

R.I.P. for C. L.-S.	23
Sour Birth	24
07.29.09. Bourg d'Oueil	25

THE GULF (FROM RIGWRECK TO DISASTER)

1 – Rigwreck / composer: Gabriel Jackson	29
Interlude 1: Word Swarm	33
2 – Love at First Sight / composer: Chris Jonas	35
Interlude 2: Word Swarm	42
3 – Dis/Aster — Oildreck / composer: Gene Coleman	44

from MEDITATIONS ON THE STATIONS OF MANSUR AL-HALLAJ

1. manners	(adab)	أدب	53
2. awe	(rahab)	رهب	54
3. fatigue	(nasab)	نسب	55
4. serach	(talab)	طلب	56
5. wonder	('ajab)	عجب	58
8. avidity	(sharah)	شره	60
9. probity	(nazah)	نزه	63
10. sincerity	(sidq)	صدق	64
11. comradeship	(rifq)	رفق	65
12. emancipation	('itq)	عتق	67
16. witnessing	(shuhud)	شهود	68
17. existence	(wujud)	وجود	70
19. labor	(kada)	كَد	71
26. presence	(hudur)	حضور	73
32. perplexity	(tahayyur)	تحيّر	74
34. patience	(tasabbur)	تصبّر	75
40. beginning	(bidaya)	بداية	77

from BARZAKH: POEMS 2000–2012

Canto Diurno 2: À / To Jack Kerouac : Ode Bilingue	85
Three Little Proses	93
Out Between	95
9/11/01	97
[Introït to my Purgatory]	98
"L'Heure Bleue"	100
Poem upon returning to these States after a 6-months absence	102
from *An Alif Baa*	
preamble to an alphabet	103
[alif]	104
[ba]	107
A poem in noon	108
The Rheumy Eye of Night	113
Another end to writing/reading #18	115
"But the ear"	116

from *Pyrenean Notebook*

"Along the coast of Sri Lanka fish feed"	117
The Sanctuary of Hands	118

from *The Fez Journals*

Bab Bou Jeloud	123
In Larache	125
"What if the birds were the shadows"	129

Canto Diurno #5

1. At the Mondrian	131
2. Lunch at La Grille (1.30 p.m.)	134

Blurb for Hütte	136
Reading Edmond Jabès	137
"I like the imp"	138
Homage to Badia Masabni	139

from THE BOOK OF U

Two for the Cormorants	143
In the dog days of summer, 3 of 'em:	144
After Basho	146
"summer's so"	147
"my cormorants"	147
"The one & only"	148
Last cor poem	151

from FOX-TRAILS, -TALES & -TROTS

A Poem in Luxembourgish on New York	157
Letter to Steichen's Ed	160

from INTERGLACIAL NARROWS

from *Læss & Found*

Elegy for Anselm Hollo	167
Avicenna to Break Up	168
Sudanese Saying	171
"Marasma redirects"	172
"our unconscious is always"	173
Haiku for the End of the World	174
The Poet's Job	174
Triggernometry of the Trinity	174
A Late Antler for Dawn Clements	175
The Art of the Fugue	176
"Purgatory is"	177
Shipping Out at 1:25 p.m. on Herman Melville's 200 birthday	178
A three-minute composition à la mode Dalachinsky to celebrate Steve	179

from *Homage to Celan*

"Earlier today I saw"	183
A Poem or something, a gift, a song, for Paul Celan at 100	184

from *Up to & Including the Virus: Diaretics 2020–2021* | 188

UNCOLLECTED POEMS

Writing / Reading #?.	207
from *An AlifBa:* ﺕ T	209
"Peace flag,"	213

xii

ACKNOWLEDGMENTS

This collection gathers selections, sometimes revised, from the following books & chapbooks published between 2000 and 2024: *Permanent Diaspora* (Duration Press, 2003); *The Rothenberg Variations* (Wild Honey Press, 2004); *learn the shadow* (unit4art, 2012); *The Gulf (between you and me)* (The Crossing, 2013); *Meditations on the Stations of Mansur al-Hallaj* (Chax Press, 2013); *Barzakh: Poems 2000–2012* (Black Widow Press, 2014); *The Book of U / Le livre des cormorans*, with Nicole Peyrafitte (Editions Simoncini, 2017); *Fox-trails, -tales & -trots: Poems & Proses* (Black Fountain Press, 2020), and *Interglacial Narrows* (ContraMundumPress, 2023).

xiii

POASIS
II

from PERMANENT DIASPORA

This afternoon Dante
will be ex-
pelled from Florence —
a good thing as how could he
have written so well
on the far-away imaginary ex-
ile of the comically divine
realms had he not known
what it meant to walk
over a cold January day's
ground frost, clod-
breaking, heart beating,
from one city to another
— to come to
this: that exile
is but the next step you take
the unknown there
where your foot comes
down
next, in
heaven or on earth
exile is when you can still
lift a foot
exile is when you are not
yet dead.

The word, the mawqif

The word is/as the *mawqif*, the station, the oasis, the momentary resting place.

The caravan of syntax discovers it, the new word, as it, the sentence, pushes into the not-yet-written, the word comes, or is given — however that happens, gift or present, possible poison in the present or present poisoned? And I stop, & if the word is new or re-newed, I will be surprised & delighted & rest in it, for a moment, then the push of ta'wil will get the sentence or line or caravan on track, no, on the trek again, into the desert ahead, in search of another oasis-word, resting place, station.

Tuesday, May 23rd 2000

full date written out
  to draw a line

between now & then,
  I.E., yesterday or last

night or this bare-
  ly past night here now

it's dawn death,
  today's early child,

time, time what we are
  inside of, banging

our heads against yet
  don't want to leave.

E.P.: heard, not seen

One.
The Pound re-
 sounds
 in these hills
 volleys of him
 mill in these ears
 all the way a
 cross two quick
 valleys
 to Exideuil.

There is a lark here too —
 don't know how to bring
 him in, except by saying
 so — but he sings when
 he wants to.

Two.
Altaforte,
 Altaforte,
 E.P. sings
 he no lark
 busy bee he
 was & brings
 you to the mark
 a restaurant table
 now *en deuil*
 of him in
 Exideuil.

Writing / Reading # 18

via JD on J-LN

the mouth is first place,
  is first,
    place of
 spacing,
  retracts from breast
 opens a cavity, cave, a-
 byss, or-
 ifice, hole,
   an o, an opening, an open
 ring.

It is touch before speech, it
  opens the first space, the
  first con-
  fusion: oral
  & buccal —

the mouth simultaneously
  place & non-place, place of a
  dis-location, gaping space
  of the *quasi permixtio* (Descartes)
  of soul & body
    ((→ etc., *Le Toucher*

try to think this mouth /
  opening together with the
  Olson/Celan
  commissure /tesserae
  matters

or : an opening, a gaping
also creates a commissure, an
angle in common, a fold.

i.e., beyond the reflexive *s'ouvre*
    se détend, it creates a
    doubling, a commonality
    (com-missure) trembling
    towards an outside, an ex-
    teriority.

(opening opens — in the middle voice

The I already two
    formed by the opening of the mouth
    makes it so
    says it so

that makes it so by saying it.
    Not round
    no circle, an
    angle.

((Angel

Or in the circus, a trapeze
    an articulation breaks
    the round.

        Break the ring-o'-roses
    to be, to say be-
    coming.
    The circle is always angular.

Circling the fire, you become
nomad by flying
off at a tangent,
at the commissure
: that possibility a
given

((If song is there first, or singing, as Nicole suggests, then its loss via
speech, its necessary loss is a breaking of that round, deeper down, in
the sound-box, a making angular, a creation of lines / of flight/. Speech
would then be the nomadicity of human sound, with song an original
at-homeness, sedentariness we escape.))

but what of Olson's
                tesserae,
                    articulations
                (laws? of the same name?
            or shards, multi-
            edged reterritorialize onto
            the roundness of escaping lines,
            of what escapes the
            commissures,

                    or the way (*der Weg,*
                        the Weg stirbt

these lines of flight articulate
            themselves?

"the desire to communicate is inversely proportionate to our real knowl-
edge of the interlocutor and directly proportional to our wish to inter-
est him in us. No need to worry about acoustics: it will always appear by
itself. What matters is distance. Whispering in the neighbor's ear quickly
tires."   Mandelstam, *De l'Interlocuteur*

what touches in not-touching ?
>the border, the untouchable,
>the always elsewhere I stalk
>I push against yet never
>touch.
>>If
>you cannot touch the
>>untouchable,
>>>but you can look
>where looking was forbidden —
a shadowy suspicion
>an aroused content
disturbing to psyche
>but "Psyche was
>a searcher in the story,
>>as a consequence of her looking
>>when looking is forbidden."   R.D., *The HD Book*

Look there, every-
>where   look at her.

>But we look to touch
>and do so in the act
>of looking —

>the desire of / in
the eye — fires
to hand to advance
>"he is looking to touch"

(touch assures being
>ear /eye /nose assure well-being   J.D., *Le toucher*
>sez Aristotle

for Gerrit Lansing at 75

The dream calls to order —
        What is due is a
          A way to-
    Do today to dance the cha cha cha
    A two-step of set
    steps up
          the Chakra-
    tree.   The Gerrit ladder
    a letter to the red
    Shah of Shah's
          The dance of trance
    formation, cha
    cha cha —

An *entre* be-
    tween two, is an *antre*-chat
          the cave of becoming
    the step in the middle
    twixt two sets

from THE ROTHENBERG VARIATIONS

Variation #1

where sun still black
    fish smells us in
    the long city
    at large in the wound
    of our curving vagina

the wind crickets
    knew you
    the stolen cavity
    wrapped heads
    splitting poison gills
    drew blood
    a sad white heart
    fully there
    searching paradise

Variation #2

& a cry neighbors there
      but he comes, my fish comes,
      emptied the death of light
      they crust the lie a
      fish comes cracks the
      hole hands disrupted
      by a spider grew out of
      air moon blood
      we roof we cold   what
      scraping   where dead
      soldiers looked was
      dark   my bed   my icicle

Variation #3

old legs & fish
>> terror sees behind mountains
>> how to be mountains

he thinks it's all up
>> I acts like overnight vase
>> your two strides

something:
>> lilies cigars asters
>> single out graves

No! granite movement flowers
>> but Bronx flowers hidden
>> in stones

Variation #6

like daytime stone with grass words
      have been constant like tin dropped
      & rendered have stood
      under & unmasked when my tears
      my forest coffin with burning wind
      comes seeking the star

spins his germany her past forms
      she buries the constant constant
      comes up comes a-crease
      the love night
      finest down finest down
      you are rolled in

& again your wings of I:
      brakemen   conductors   eagles

I's now eyes

Variation #9

ice hooks
>meat hooks
>white & black hooks

the air listens
>no one sits burning
>we are all
>the dancer walks
>on air
>whose will raised tresses
>we have seen domains
>he possesses
>listen to what's on
>tender hooks dreams
>fashioned in meat
>licking we sit
>face to face beneath a dream
>of mercy toward a sea
>drowns every black
>hook feeling
>a face wandering beneath

Note: This sequence of poems was composed to honor Jerome Rothenberg on his 70th birthday & was first read at the Poetry Project at St. Mark's Church celebration for that occasion, held on Wednesday, December 12th, 2001. The poems are composed following a détournée +7 method: each poem is based on word material (each 7th word) of the first 15 poems in JR's first & latest books. The arrangement is my own, as are excisions, additions, subtractions & divisions.

from LEARN THE SHADOW

R.I.P. for C. L.-S.

The self is
       "haïssable,"
       detestable —

       the man who just
       lost his self
       said
long ago
       adding that
       where there is

"pas de moi"
       no me, no I

there will be
       a nothingness

or an us,
       no, he said "and"

"un rien et
       un nous:"

which this morning
       (pardon the departed)
       I want to translate as

a noos
       & a noose.

Sour Birth

dear Anselm,
      there may be a typo
      in that poem:
      the line "Just a sour birth"
      should read
      "Just as our birth"
      unless the poem wanted it to be
      the other way around.

07.29.09. Bourg d'Oueil

to learn the shadow
    shapes of the birds
    of prey in a late

sky — while the coals
    in the kanoun turn
    from black to white

having glowed through
    a blood-like red
    — & flies drink this ink.

THE GULF
(FROM RIGWRECK TO DISASTER)

1 – Rigwreck / composer: Gabriel Jackson

Interlude 1: Word Swarm

2 – Love at First Sight / composer: Chris Jonas

Interlude 2: Word Swarm

3 – Dis/Aster — Oildreck / composer: Gene Coleman

From *Rigwreck* by Gabriel Jackson; text by Pierre Joris.

Rigwreck

A THROW
>> What do we know, what can we know?
>>>> OF THE DICE
>> of science, of love?
>>>>>> only the facts, that is to say
>>>>>> only effects
>>>>>>> NEVER
>> Can this happen
NEVER even if, can this happen
>>> in science, in love
>>>> EVEN WHEN CAST
>> Indra's net of love,

*

EVEN WHEN CAST
>>> Money's net of stone
what do we know, what can we know?
>> What has caused this gulf
between water & oil, you & me
>>>> IN ETERNAL CIRCUMSTANCES
>> (no circumstances are eternal,
AT THE HEART OF
>>> of this rigwreck
What will we know?
>> We know only effects / have to choose
the causes

*

A SHIPWRECK at the heart that the
gulf widens

between water & oil, you & me
fish & water, me & you
that the
Abyss
between water & water, you & you
me & me, oil & fish
widened then whitened
there is slack growing
raging underwater in the heart
underheart in the water
on the brain

✻

what we know is oil & water don't mix
what we know is fish & oil don't mix

what we know is you & I have to mix
what we know is you & I have to live

under an incline
clinamen of a warming clime
an angle not an angel tells us
me & you want to live
even if despair desperately soars
& gets an angry rise

✻

from the phantom pain of its own planet's sore
broken wing
a second-hand angel singing Ecce Homo,
Ecce Homo, though not so Sapiens,
conscious liar,
beforehand relapsed, liar, liar,
not released from wrongly steering
the flight of this planetary love affair

                    no use repressing the outbursts
                         of this lethal love affair
                              cleaving the bounds
*

of this oily love affair
                at the root of greed
                     set the rig afloat
                          a ship finally a ship
                               the impossible change
              for deep inside weighs the admission of impending disaster
*

the shadow hidden in the depth
                by this by this arrogance this arrogance
          at the root of greed this arrogance
                at the root of arrogance
                     this love this love for more
                          a more always spelled out in money
*

blows the rig up this morning
        will blow the world up tomorrow
            there is no alternate sail
                ship earth in space / space ship earth
                     the only raft for dumb sapiens
who has to learn to love
this imperfect raft
there is no alternate sail
*

dumb sapiens has to learn love
         has to learn to adjust
                has to learn to look   to the spread
the spreading of disaster
         has to learn to jump
                its yawning depth

as great as any abyss

                                between you & me

          the hull of a rig
                    the hull of a ship

*

careening from side to side
          turns over & is for a moment cathedral
                    burning church of the worship of money
brightly floating death flaunting love
                              rigwreck rigwreck
a catastrophe here now,
                    the circumstances local & global
          not eternal only this now
cannot grasp the hawser
                              opens a gulf
                                   between life & death

*

a millimeter uncrossable
          a BP centipede monster
at the heart of this rigwreck
                    abolish   abolish
abolished responsibility
                    Moloch, Moloch
Moloch —
                    rules, Moloch
                                        rules
all rules broken when Moloch rules.

Interlude 1:

WORD SWARM APRIL 20 2010

joint military operation
Iraqi American forces killed two senior
al-Qaeda leaders
Abu Ayyub al-Masri, & Abu Omar al-Baghdadi
News broke explosion at 11 p.m. EST on BP's
Deepwater Horizon oil rig
safe house in Thar-Thar in the province of
Salaheddin
umbrella group, Islamic State of Iraq
radical Sunni militant groups
General Raymond Odierno said significant blow
to al-Qaeda
24 people killed 2 separate suicide bombing
attacks in Peshawar
A schoolboy victim attacks take death toll
to 73 in three days, after two blasts in the
city of Kohat killed 49 people during the
weekend
News broke an explosion occurred at 11 p.m. EST
on BP's Deepwater Horizon oil rig in the
Gulf of Mexico
A magnitude 5.2 earthquake hit
Western Australian mining town
Kalgoorlie-Boulder this morning.
Long Island teen guilty of murdering
Ecuadorian immigrant Marcelo Lucero.
Toyota pays a record $16.4 million fine to the
US government over allegations that the
automaker concealed defects in its vehicles
– sticky pedal
NATO service members died bomb attack
army base southern Afghanistan.

From "Love at First Sight" by Chris Jonas; text by Pierre Joris.

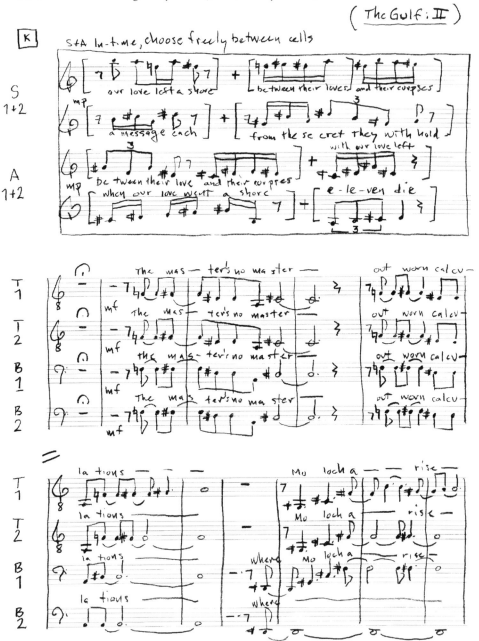

Love at First Sight

CHOIR:

> THE MASTER is no master
> the master is a corp   a corpse a corporation
> beyond outworn calculations
> where Moloch where Moloch arisen
> is a manoeuvre with age-
> less scorn for you & me
> scorn for love / love forgotten
> the master is absent
> now present here only Dewey
> could have gripped the helm once
> upon a time & called his mates
> now locked into the assistant driller's shack's C chair
> can his love hear him

SOLO (Dewey's voice):

> Thirty years offshore
> & I can smell a rat
> leaving a rig, I can, I do right now —
> I'm toolpusher, not master,
> should sleep but follow
> inauspicious orders
> tomorrow's another day, night's growing darker
> something's wrong here, something's off
> shouldn't follow inauspicious orders
> It is night / the only light
> is tomorrow is Sheri

Sheri my love a gulf between us
   my message reaches across a gulf
     awaits you listen listen
       left it this morning at first light
O why am I not ashore I knew
   the bosses would lie would cut
       corners until from this conflagration . . .

CHOIR:
     at his feet mud overflows the rig floor
       shoots through the derrick
   the blowout preventer's does not act
the well's blown out
   Dewey dead now in this conflagration
on the no way unanimous horizon
      end of the horizon
       of the deepwater horizon
a Gulf prepares itself
    the fist would grip it
  will swallow the tossed & burning rig
as one threatens destiny & the winds, the elements all
     eleven die
  the one Number which can be no other
    eleven die
     their Spirit hurled
       into tempestuous fire gas explosions
    nothing can seal the gap nothing can go proudly
  eleven die
love left ashore a Gulf
      between their loves & their corpses
    eleven die
     eleven die.

SOLO (Female Voice / Sheri):

> Dewey got pretty hot
>> Dewey never—ever—ever
>>> loses his temper — never, ever, ever.
> If he really believed this could have happened,
>> he'd never, never let them do it.
> Calls at 9 a.m. each morning
>> missed his call that morning,
>>> phone didn't ring, he left
>>>> a message I deleted as
>> I knew he was coming home
>>> knew he was coming home.

CHOIR:

> Don't hesitate
>> cut off from the secret they withhold
>>> cadavers that will not wash ashore
> caught rather than dressed
>> now in shrouds of lethal
> oil & dispersant pearls
> old madmen play the game on behalf of the waves
>> one surges over the chief toolpusher
> a directly shipwrecked
> all-American love story flows over:
>> of the man no submissive graybeard
>>> who just liked being home,
>> ancestrally huntin', fishin', playin' on his tractor
>>> not to unclench his hand
> She without a ship
>> a small place in Ohio, no matter where vainly there was:
>>> Kmart in walking distance,
>>>> mall twenty minutes by car.

They met when he drove up to the local Kerr
    gas station where Sheri worked.

SOLO (Female Voice /Sheri):
It was love at first sight
    We had the old-time Coca-Cola coolers.
        He reached in for one he was sittin' there
            we were talkin' that was it...
                He had this smile. It would make you melt.
                Love at first sight.

CHOIR:
        Contracted before & above the worthless wellhead showed
She was 18 & he was 21 when they got married
        an all-American love story
           the legacy of his disappearance
    yet back then no gulf between them
        to some unknown the ulterior immemorial demon.

SOLO (Female Voice):
    It was love at first sight.
        When we got married so young
           everyone was looking for a baby.
              There wasn't one.
                We were just in love.

CHOIR:
From dead & narrow lands
    induced / seduced
        by an old man toward this supreme lethal
           conjunction with probability
this morning she expected him home

sister called at 5 a.m. said turn on the t.v.
she knew right away that he'd be dead.
Even his boyish shadow
caressed & polished, drained & washed
not to return wave-softened
unyielding bones stripped off
lost among the debris

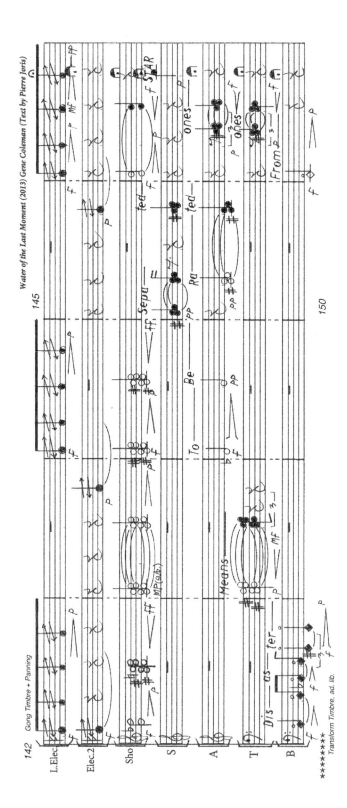

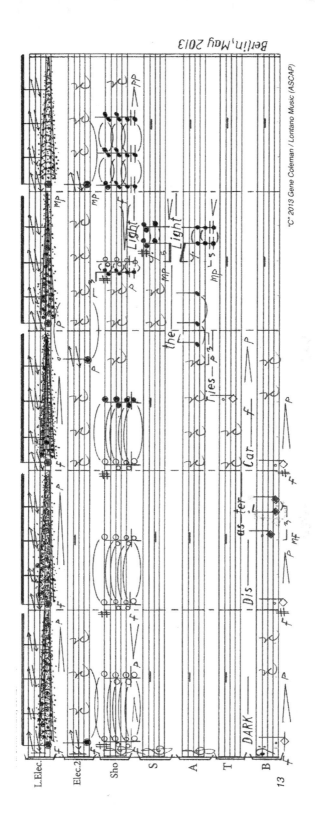

Interlude 2:
WORD SWARM 20 APRIL 2010

death toll of foreign soldiers in 2010 to 166 in
Afghanistan
McLaren driver Jenson Button won the Chinese Grand Prix
re-open the skies over Europe
ash from a volcano in Iceland
a high pressure here & a low pressure there
News broke that an explosion occurred at 11 p.m. EST
on BP's Deepwater Horizon oil rig
in the Gulf of Mexico southeast of Venice
the jet stream came down, spun around, &
then went back up through the Straits of Gibraltar
amphibians, reptiles, mammals, bird & fish species
Remembering Columbine 11 years ago
celebrate National Park Week
largest subtropical wilderness
showdown Senate financial reform
Zephyrs top Express in 11 innings
Today's Money Word is deflation
BIG Oil Rig Explosion Off Louisiana Coast,
11 to 15 People Missing, Infernal Blaze
trust leaked away with the Tritium
bar NEPA analysis of climate change impact
Being fat is bad for your brain
erratic, potentially fatal heart rhythms
defibrillator responsibility the Guidant Corporation
short-circuit & fail
"Nobody is being held accountable."
Google criticized privacy practices
the privacy rights of the world's citizens forgotten
stricter enforcement of title IX
Twain's last words
Best Nonholiday Quarter for Apple
Taliban sniper fire lethality rates drop
Peter Steele "Life is killing me" is dead
no ban on animal cruelty videos

Off Louisiana Coast, 11 to 15 People Missing,
Statoil Committed to Oil Sands
Bush warcrimes on off broadway
Miami Condo Sales rise
Oil Rig Explosion Infernal Blaze
boxer hangs himself in jail
Reds pitcher Volquez suspended
Tuesday, April 20
News broke that an explosion occurred at 11 p.m. EST
on BP's Deepwater Horizon oil rig in the Gulf of Mexico
52 miles southeast of the Louisiana port of Venice.
According to the Coast Guard, 11 to 15 crew members
were reported missing
of the total 126 workers aboard the rig
at the time of the blast.

Dis/Aster — Oildreck

Disaster: not thought gone awry

when all this first started
  my body broke out into real bad rashes
    my eyes my face my neck my chest my back my shoulders
big giant holes on the back of my legs,
  holes the size of a #2 pencil
    looked just like the holes
      in the fish
        in the lab
          on the screen

Gulf: from Greek κόλπος (kólpos) m. [masculine], a bosom, from Proto-European *bheu-ə- :"to swell, bend, curve"

What have you done to know disaster?

we went to detox —— December 11 to January 12
  the children feel much better now
    Alina still has bad days
      she may never be 100%.
my little boy is doing fantastic,
  my husband's better &
    I'm feeling better too . . .
  I've shelled out $40.000

Gulf: A hollow place in the Earth

Disaster: on the side of forgetting

we did blue crab before BP
> *but since BP*
>> *we don't blue crab anymore*

Gulf: an abyss, a bottomless or unfathomed depth

Disaster: care for the minuscule

> *all of a sudden we had shrimp*
>> *with what they call black gill disease*
>>> *if they were blue would it be blue gill disease?*

we've had shrimp
> *with growth on them*
>> *we've had had fish with growths on'em*

Gulf: a deep Chasm, a steep-sided rift, gap or fissure, a large difference of opinion

Disaster: sovereignty of the accident

the Vietnamese & the Cambodian communities
> *a really tough time being hired on*
>> *the great language barrier:*
>>> *90% of the information put out*
>>>> *in the first 60 days was English only*

Gulf: a basin, from Latin "bacca" wine jug, Welsh "baich," load, burden, Irish "bac," hindrance

45

In relation to disaster, one dies too late

> *the herring came in to mature*
> > *dropped on the seafloor dead*
> *compromised immune system couldn't*
> > *fight off a parasite, a natural bacteria*

Gulf: a rock formation scooped out by water erosion

Disaster disorients the absolute

> *grey amberjack, king mackerel, red snapper, mangrove snapper,*
> *caught off shore when we gutted*
> > *had black sludge inside their stomachs*
> > *crossed stomach walls*
> > *made holes in the meat*
> *you could literally physically see it with the naked eye*

Gulf: (obsolete) that which swallows, the gullet

Disaster comes and goes

> *the blue runners will hit the oil*
> *off the top of the water, the droplets,*
> > *larger fish get it inside of them eating*
> > > *their normal food source and then*
> *it's gone, it's gone it's not there anymore, it doesn't exist*

Gulf: that which swallows irretrievably, a whirlpool, a sucking eddy

Disaster: nomad disarray

the whole circle of life
in the Gulf things that we don't eat
      whales dolphins turtles all this different stuff
if it kills everything then what do we do?

    an overflow, people flooding
      the area all the way from Arkansas & all over the US
and they were able to come down here with boats
    because they weren't from here,
      they took some of our fishermen & put them over
in Alabama
      & took some Alabama fishermen & put them over here.
And what it was all about was
    controlling the images!

Gulf: A large deposit of ore (rock containing metal or gems) in a
lode (a vein of ore in boundaries, a rich supply, also see water-course,
lodestone, lodestar)

Disaster means to be separated from one's star

if everybody got up and said "enough is enough"
—— there is power in numbers ——
then we may be able to move
& really get it cleaned up ——
—— it is still leaking
—— mine said they ran through oil all day yesterday
oil & dispersant
in the water the dispersant
when they first put it out looked
like sand from the Sahara desert
into contact with the oil it gets foamy slimy nasty
on top of the water

Gulf: from Greek κόλπος (kólpos) m. [masculine], anatomically, vagina and/or atrium of the heart.

Disaster lies on the other side of danger

dark disaster carries the light

takes care of everything

Notes

— The first two sections of the work are partial writing-throughs of Stéphane Mallarmé's poem *A Throw of the Dice*, using both Daisy Alden & my translations. Despite being usually called the first "abstract" poem of the modern avant-garde, that poem tells a story: that of a shipwreck & the drowning of its captain.

— A number of the spoken phrases in the second section are taken from interviews with Sheri Revette by Antonia Juhasz in the latter's book *Black Tide* (Wiley, 2011), talking of her husband, Dewey Revette, a driller killed in the Deepwater Horizon disaster on April 20 2010. Sheri tells the story of their love & life together and the moments after Sherri learns of her husband's death.

— Chris Jonas at some point asked me for "news chatter," a "word swarm," scattered words not in the poem as such but yet relevant, which he could use to make sounds with. I have gathered my gleanings of news chatter into two ticker tape-like "Interludes" inserted between the sections of the sequence.

— In the third section, the spoken words in italics are taken from an interview I conducted in New Orleans in February 2012 with Kindra Arnesen, fisherwoman, wife of a fisherman, mother, activist, cofounder of the Coastal Heritage Society, a feisty & powerful voice in the fight for justice after the Gulf disaster, as willing to take on local prejudices as BP or the US Government.

— The texts of the bold-faced "frames" around her words use disaster definitions/phrasings from Maurice Blanchot's book *L'écriture du désastre* & etymological definitions of the word "gulf" from various dictionaries.

from MEDITATIONS ON THE STATIONS OF MANSUR AL-HALLAJ

for Miles

> *Each Station's its own gift:*
> *some you'll get,*
> *some you won't.*

> *Then the exile went into*
> *the desert, embraced*
> *it all.*

> *He found nothing familiar*
> *or useful there — not on*
> *the mountain, not on the plain.*

1. manners　　(adab)　　أدب

what is the manner
　　　　I mean the matter

with you standing
　　　　there in the desert?

Take your hands
　　　　out of your pockets

the desert has no manners
　　　　but many pockets

which is no excuse for your
　　　　lack of know-how

when it comes to sharing
　　　　this last pinch of

hot sand & mica
　　　　hides as lint

in the pockets
　　　　of your heart

2. awe (rahab) رهب

        the awe is in gawking
    when you see it

it scares you
    where it's the unseen

you seem to want to care
    for even though

it scars you to face the
    awe that is not

in the thing or the it
    but between the two

it's the relation a
    we can be

3. fatigue   (nasab)   نسب

tiredness of the beginning
        century, go into it
        the fatigue, let it

round off the all too nervy
        edges, loosen the tie
        die the saffron

heart take heart in fat
        & gay, no sob but
        reinvent the hammock,

act with languor as
        you slip beneath
        the tent, oh Sheikh.

4. serach   (talab)   طلب

there is confusion inside
      an era the terms
      are demands on
      the table.

que sera sera. arch labels, typos
      reach high demands
      resignation no better than search.
      desire.

search your words for the con
      of fusion. make letters
      stand out even if
      they shiver.

it is snow tales this
      dawn. words like
      palm trees are in high
      demand. desist.

2.

      whenever one enjoys favor
      all actions so many tokens.
      demonstration is search
      and his neglect

thereof is "resignation"
        no better than search
        for search is a principle
        cannot be neglected

impotence is the
        annihilation
        of the faculty
        of search.

5. wonder ('ajab) عجب

and you'll find
    or wander if you don't
    and if you do
    wander to wonder

a wonder is a jab in the head
    a wonder pries the heart ajar

or is a done thing too often
    blinds us to what's left
    to do.

so he walks on water.
    whatever. a miracle in other
    words is a wonder. *Ein*
    Wunder.

Some one sore and wounded.
    A real god or wonder-
    worker.

The loaves and the wine
    at the wedding — a neat
    trick but one we'd need

to be able to do anywhere
    all the time. we can,
    or could — that wonder would

be called just
     distribution
     of the world's wealth.

8. avidity   (sharah)   شره

the opposite of sharing
       does not invite

a city is full of it
       the old country

slogan
       ora et labora

has only its
       rhyme scheme left

after the laughter
       the fat of greed

dissolves
       a charred remembrance

a *haram*
       on the greedy king

of kings. if
       you don't

believe go
       to the avidity

primer. this is
        a method

not a product.
        use it with any kit.

2.

The word
        crossed over

lost its moral
        on the way

to the lab,
        hear in it

the dissociation-
        dependent strength

of any acid or base.
        a protein-shark

in uncooked egg whites
        hogs the biotin

we need to live
        & needs bacteria, yeasts,

molds, algae,
        some plant life.

of course it can be
        bottled and we

beat any lower price.
        It's all in the

brand name and we've
        got that sewn up.

9. probity   (nazah)   نزه

Lament its absence
　　among those who govern.

10. sincerity   (sidq)   صدق

you could try standing
     beside your word

but which one of the
     many thousands?

11. comradeship   (rifq)   رفق

we stand here
    riffing on

comradeship
    tho we don't

know the first or
    the last letter

of it. tho we are
    — or have to be —

in the middle of
    what Creeley called

the company — those
    we break

bread with,
    even if it turns

out to be
    poisoned

fish as we did that once—
    the comradeship goes on

in the particle com links
    us to the common

& a manifesto of equality
      & we will keep standing

here in the wind on the corner
      where desert and city meet

we will keep standing here
      our hands in your pockets

always riffing even
      if some of us

are spectral
      comrades now,

as it is
      our job to be close

to those gone
      to bring back their news

talk through
      their voices

we are all
      they have

left — squeezed
      as they are

in the tight fists
      hands make
in our pockets.

12. emancipation   ('itq)   عتق

What's tough is the final hard
        qaaf ق following lit, how to

get from the t — its plosive
        air expellent end — to the

qaaf ق way further back, how to
        emancipate an old habituated

throat to associate consonants
        to make them strange

bedfellows on a bed
        of new air. how to breathe

between, without pre-
        cipitation, no pat solutions,

no lit conforming ease,
        to learn anew how to breathe.

16. witnessing   (shuhud)   شهود

1.

no, I don't want to.
    it is all you can do.

who are you to tell
    me what I did. you

saw nothing. you
    were not there. I

was. He or she are
    the necessary third

let them tell me or
    you what the all is

you or me did do.
    no one witnesses.

2.

so, you don't want to.
    it is all I can do.

who am I to tell
    you what I did. You heard

nothing. my eyes
          were closed, you

saw nothing either I
          was not there or you

were and what if so I
          closed my ears.

Why should you want to.
          You heard nothing.

I saw it all. He or
          she are the necessary

third party, she said
          now I've heard it all.

17. existence (wujud) وجود

1.

if the talk is
       of a three-pronged fork

he translates it as
       "a three-pronged fork"

so that the literal
       existence of the thing

does not get lost
       in translation.

2.

I came here screaming
       they tell me maybe

worried that I'll leave
       as loudly or lowly

but there is no high exit
       only a sinking

out of existence —
       an impossible witnessing.

19. labor   (kada)   كَدّ

to each day
     its labor

isn't sufficient
     & is certain-

ly not wisdom maybe
     a laborious essay

to veil the condition
     we claim as ours.

à chaque jour
     suffit sa peine

to unveil this
     morning's condition

translates *peine*
     as labor

thinks of *cada*
     as each

in spanish now
     of a tail

or cauda as in
      what is the

coda of labor?
      asleep in

fatigues conned
      again by what M

had cleared: labor
      is not work

work is sufficient
      if you can

get it
      work at

the great daily
      unworking

26. presence   (hudur)   حضور

always comes before
    the mirror reveals it.

it is the abstraction
    we live in. "A body

is a sea, it is always
    in movement, always

in movement, it precedes
    us & it follows us" (Adonis).

the present is how we
    think of it afterward.

is the in-between
    we cannot grasp

the barzakh we travel,
    archipelago of the everyday —

except for the last
    & the one after.

32. perplexity   (tahayyur)   تحيّر

a perp in a city
　　　　is the old lex

law & order
　　　　perplexes me

34. patience   (tasabbur)   تصبّر

whose patience? the mother's
immense, eternal

patience for her child,
an absolute of species, it is

life-long (her
life's length, that is)

or the child's frayed
patience with the aging

parent — the mother already
beyond time, out of time,

timelessness of forgetting
alzheimer's folly

I forget I forget she says
be patient with me, child

even as I am impatient with
my own memory, mother

says I hear does she
hear what

she says what I say
     the distance of impatience

with her now who am I
     to tell her.

"This is fatal, the disease
     is called Remember"   [R.K., "The Death Goliath"]

40. beginning   (bidaya)   بداية

the end is in the beginning
    the end is the beginning

the troops have left
    have the troops left

I can finish what I began
    when they first invaded

& promised not to end
    until they all had left

the troops have left
    have the troops left

too easy to claim
    an end as a new

beginning, nothing begins
    anew, nothing ends for keeps

except the lives of those killed by
    the bullets put money into

the pockets of those who
    sold you the war, those who

never had their hands in
        their (own) pockets those who

never stood in any desert except
        their own hearts' alkali wastes

& the lint in their pockets soaked
        through with spent blood now

pulled from pockets & flicked
        onto the desert's

face, thousands of lives
        stubbed out like Camel butts

the troops have left
        have the troops left

U.S. you no Orestes
        Iraq you no Argos   *Najem Wali*

Sartre's flies did not leave
        the lord thereof keeps buzzing

both but Sumer shall rise again
        Baghdad will be Baghdad again

others who be the truth, al-haqq,
        will be put to life & to death other

poets will write & celebrate
        oh now then let's

begin the beguine
        bedaya the beduin

bring back the sound of a music so tender
        a night of desert splendor

bring back a memory of green
        in a rapture so serene

that what were raging fires
        now are glowing memory embers

desire not dead
        desire not dead

& if the city hurt you
        walk out into the deep

pockets of the desert
        the place we all came from

the place we shall all return to.
        Mansur, Mansur, lead the dance!

POST-FACE

I started this sequence of poems shortly after the U.S. invaded Iraq, somehow wanting to ward off, or hold at bay, the utter destruction of the people & the city of Baghdad, one of the greatest old cities in the history of humanity. Years earlier, when living in Algeria & reading up on sufism & related matters, I had been fascinated by the big four-volume work the French Orientalist scholar Louis Massignon has dedicated to Mansur al-Hallaj, the tenth-century revolutionary poet, sufi teacher & thinker. Al-Hallaj had been executed (after much torture) in Baghdad on 6 March 922, after eleven years spent in a Baghdad jail. His crime had been to have said "ana al-haqq" or "I am the truth" — an expression that traditionally names one of the attributes of god — something neither the political or religious powers of the day could condone, even from a very famous & highly loved & esteemed visionary poet & teacher. I did not own the Massignon, so quickly started to scour the internet for al-Hallaj material & came up with a very basic — anonymous, as far as I could discover — list in English & Arabic of forty concepts taken, from al-Hallaj's teachings. Deciding to use the found list as titles for a sequence of forty poems, I started to work — but felt that the last one, wonderfully called "beginning, bedaya," would have to be held back until the last U.S. troops had left Iraq. I progressed quickly enough & by 2007 a chapbook of the first 21 poems were published by Christopher Rizzo's Anchorite Press. I wrote on, the poems now often becoming longer, then stopped at 39 & waited until the first days of 2012 when I was finally able to write the last one.

A few years into the writing I was able to acquire Stéphane Ruspoli's excellent 2007 book, *Le livre "Tawasin" de Hallaj* (Albouraq, Beirut), & could thus verify that these were the "40 stations of Moses" from part II of al-Hallaj's book, the section entitled "Les quarante stations de Moïse et l'appel devant le buisson ardent." On the face of it, Ruspoli's translation seems to propose 43, while his original Arab text seems to come to 41 — a mystery I have not yet been able to resolve. This is not the place to analyze Al-Hallaj's dense & ecstatic, allusive & rhetorical, occult & revelatory *Kitab al Tawasin*, or *Book of Tawasin*. Suffice it to point to the poetic letter magic of the complex, playful & untranslatable title word "tawasin," a word made up from the Arabic letter "ta," emphatic "t," the conjunction "wa," meaning "and," & the letter "sin," our "s."

But such discrepancies are to be expected, & it is probably in the fissures between miscounts, recounts, etymologies, misreadings, neologisms, etc. that much of the poetic force of language resides. I have therefore not either been too concerned about my "found" list, which obviously contains its own shares of such "problems." For example, the translation of station 3, "nasab," as "fatigue," is very odd, to say the least, as the Arabic term rather refers to kinship & genealogy. For the next station, the translation of the Arabic word "talab" is mistyped as "serach" when the obvious correct form is "search." Not only have I not corrected such mistakes but I've consciously

80

tried to integrate them into the composition of the poem, at least wherever or whenever that felt needed &/or appropriate.

I called the book *Meditations on the Stations of Mansur al-Hallaj*, where the word "station" is a translation of the Arabic word "mawqif" (plural: "mawāqif"), a concept I had written on in *A Nomad Poetics*, defining it as "the pause, the stop-over, the rest, the stay of the wanderer between two moments of movement, two runs, two sites, two places, two states." It is a complex term which I analyze at some length in that book, & I am quite aware that in a rigidly scholarly sense it should not be used in relation to al-Hallaj, as the term mawqif was coined & used by the slightly later 10th century mystic & writer Niffari (died ~965) — & one of whose books is called *al-mawâqif (The Stations.)* I felt that the term corresponded rather exactly to those concepts & to my work with them. Furthermore, Ruspoli too uses the term "stations" in the book mentioned above. The Moroccan poet Mohammed Bennis has recently written a fascinating essay, a defense & illustration of my use of the concept of "mawqif," which the interested reader can check out in the recently published *Pierre Joris: Cartographies of the In-Between*.

I dedicate this work to my son Miles, who turned eleven the year the Iraq war started, a war that is thus the first one he consciously experienced in his life. I cannot even say "may it be the only one," as several wars have broken out since & are raging on. May he & his generation be spared the worst of these totally unnecessary lethal inhuman insanities.

January 6, 2012
Bay Ridge

from BARZAKH: POEMS 2000–2012

Canto Diurno 2

À / To Jack Kerouac : Ode Bilingue

l'à-

> *tout* Kerouac
> deux as
> sans volant,
> son cosas
> de tristessa, la
> vida goes
> on as I
> start 6:06 a.m.
> 23 June 1999 from
> Joey's Riverside Restaurant
> dawn sunny side up
> in truckstop 23
> (nous aimons fermer la Noël)
> mais ce n'est que la
> pré-Saint Ti Jean
> a day for Jack
> lapsed Buddhist
> hitchhiked 1,000 miles
> histoire de
> t'apporter du vin
> histoire de
> mourir /
> il y a 30 ans
> il ya 45 ans
> tu écrivais (235 Chorus) :
> "Je sais que je suis mort.

Je ne camperai pas. Je suis mort maintenant.
    Qu'est-ce que j'attends pour disparaître? . . ."
30 years ago — & aujourd'hui
ici aux chiottes
c'est écrit:
"Colfax Driver Sucks"
(dans la bouche, oui,
dans le cul, non,
la sexpol de Jack)
graffiti & café
une carte dé-
roule la route
drive to Lowell
dark shades in bright
a.m. rising
sun, in the house
        of,
            Jack's nights
mon teenage dream
of America
            mon truck stop blues
un blues for Jack
gone these thirty years now
& Allen gone
& William gone
mais reste Gregorio
in Nueva Yorkio
spitting smack in the face
of death,
reste Sanders
à Woodstock workin'
for the city

et puis
Claude à Binghamton
careening down
Carotid Bypass —
Et donc,
il n'est jamais trop tard, Jack,
repasser sur ta tombe,
passer en trombe,
trompe l'œil ou trompe-la-mort,
trompette de la mort à une
heure et demi de voiture
coup de volant coup de volonté
Jack n'en avait plus au paradis
des trompes en Floride, trop
croyables Florides aux
glauques troupeaux,
il s'est heurté aux tentacules de
l'archange mère
sous l'horizon des mers abandonnées
& tu ne l'as pas trouvé
"le Saint Lait Intérieur
que Damema, Mère des Bouddhas
donna à tous." (chorus 225)
Tu gagnas et perdis les
plages des Grandes Plaines
vagues Kansas vague Nebraska
et vogue la galère bière
Saint Jack le sait:
Gabrielle le préfère
mort-éthylique que
suceur de bites juives
et Jack embrasse son karma-

87

sixpack — Ah!
comment se conduire
sans s'étendre méli-mélo,
how to drive through
all the sad-sack
comings & goings
& not back up memory
's cul-de-sac,
même si
Maggie est le nom
de la serveuse fatiguée
aux bas nylon cache-varices
au show-avaries
sous le signe :
  Cashier / Take Out
Signe pour
101enzoi immédiat, sun-
struck in Plaza 23 & à 8:15
arrêt à Blanchard MOBIL station
of no cross I hope
along Mass Turnpike la
table en bois d'où je veux t'écrire
déjà inscrite :

"Opinion is a flitting thing
   L'opinion est chose passagère
But truth, outlasts the Sun —
   Mais la vérité, dure plus que le soleil —
If then we cannot own them both —
   Si donc nous ne pouvons les posséder toutes deux —
Possess the oldest one —
    Possédons la plus ancienne —"

Emily Dickinson
     "Poème utilisé avec permission"
     nom gravé sur le banc sous mon cul,
     le soleil, Jack, est le plus vieux
     de tous, mais comment le
     posséder? Ce chaud
     matin d'été
     vertes forêts & collines
     du Massachusetts
     plis sur plis tout autour
     de la voiture,
          open as I ride,
     sweet tender light
     green,
          gobbles us up,
     in intimations of
     la même vieille
     mortality.

*   *   *

Walked downtown Lowell
     to high school
     (insert picture here)
     to monument
     (insert picture here)
     & now at 112 Gorham
     once Nicky's
     & thus Jack's watering hole
     now Ricardo's Eye-
     talian restaurant —
     R's father, ex-mayor of Lowell,
     now 82, is mentioned in *On*
     The Road,
          Sez Ricardo's manager,

Qui me montre
dans le nouveau restaurant
le vieux bar
dont la surface
si tu penches la tête
à un certain angle
montre encore
l'impact des bottes
pits of boots
once danced
w/ Jack in atten-
      dance
ce qui reste:
Ricardo sells, on tap,
  de la Stella
Artois, celle-là,
mais me fila
Mary Sampas'
phone number au journal —
ne l'ai pas appelée,
  walked over to Jack's
  old Canuck St. Jean
  Baptiste cathedral on
  Merrimack, qui s'appelle
  maintenant l'Eglise Nuestra Senora
  del Carmen, mais verrouillée,
  tu ne t'y retrouverais pas,
  Jack, ce qui était
  Franco-Canadien / Irlandais
  est Dominicain / Vietnamien,
  je suis revenu vers la voiture
  passant près du "Paradise Diner"
  (insérer image ici)

qui donna peut-être le nom
du héros de *Sur La Route*,
à moins que ce ne fut la phrase de
Ginsberg, "Sad Paradise!"
Triste Paradis, indeed, ce Lowell
où j'ai conduit jusqu'au coin
de Pawtucket & School
l'orphelinat Franco-ricain
son horrible grotto qui t'effrayait
      (insérer image ici)
drive-through stations of the cross
life-size Katholick Guilt,
l'horreur, l'horreur,
pauvre Ti Jean caught & killed
by that trip
malgré les Golden Buddhist Scriptures
of other Eternities,
drove out to cemetery
j'ai foncé jusqu'au cimetière
kneeled in front of
the plaque, 2 cannettes vides,
1 empty sweet peach brandy bottle
1 twisted fork,
2 notes gribouillées: Dear Jack . . .
3 candle butts
etcetera
drove back Al-
bany-way
wondering where to insert
Yves Buin's line
"J'ai croisé un visionaire
      et nous avons fait quelques pas."
Le pas, le pas

le suivre au, ne pas
n'est-ce pas là
la difficulté —
Comment trouver
cette forme sauvage
"la seule forme
qui contienne ce que j'ai
à dire"
pour écrire des lignes parfaites comme
"welkin moon wrung salt
upon the tides of come-on nights — "
ou encore comme tu
l'as écrit à Allen: "Forget
the facts and think
of the things, *all* the
things." — "Oublie les faits
et pense
aux choses, à toutes les
choses."
Et là je pense à toi,
Jack, la chose-Kerouac,
la prose-Kerouac, l'amer-
ique.

Three Little Proses

I. From genotype to phenotype

In the beginning they say was the rod. And, I say, it was double from the word go: the cool black on white word of the book, and the hot and fast word of the radio. And the word on the radio let me cold to begin with, while the word on the page was what asked me to light up my nights — with a flashlight under the covers.

II.

Kafka's take that the downfall of Babel had to do with bad foundations, shoddy architecture suggests that those who built it were originally tent-dwellers, nomads, & that the destruction was a nomad god's way of criticizing the attempt at bricked-in sedentariness — it is after the tower has collapsed that the people went back to their travelin' ways, which the priests of the Bible of course try to push as a curse: "So YHWH scattered them over the face of the earth, and they had to stop building the city." *De la récupération, pure et simple.* The end of that chapter of Genesis brings in Abraham, who chooses to become the ultimate nomad, leaving Ur, to wander, not so much in pursuit of an earthly paradise but following a calling, a spiritual direction (or maybe just a word voiced on the radio) — a spiritual direction he does not know whereto it will lead him, rather than some well-established route of transhumance.

III.

from "trans" + lat. "Humus" *ground* cf. *dhghem* —

bridegroom
       chamomile
              humble
homage
homicide
      human

Out Between

"this is happening" she said
in the muddle purge
oratory. can
Ned, not I, in
fuse the middle
stand. ground. class.

a container trans-
parent sentences.

the two you. The to
you. The us of
things, the rex of
things no rex.
unqueened anorexia.

freeze and rotate
he flips forward through
the gymnastic hour:
rotate with feet in bucket
arms on horse.

a container. body
in the middle,
the muddle.

into the middle
I insert the beginning.
you'll come to it.

I start anywhere.
        wolf it down from
        out between Jekyll & Hide.
        The conjunction an elegant
        glyph, glosses where we are.
        here & there. now & then.

9/11/01

to be written
  when the
  time comes:

this moment,
  this second
  cuts in be-

tween in two.
  It will be the —
  where to breathe

the or a o-
  pen pore
  riots of air

that second
  always second
  rift in time

marks time
  for breath, gash
  curled high in air.

      Albany, 7:20 a.m.

[Introït to my Purgatory]

the biggest lie is
        that we were kicked out
           of Paradise.

No one kicked us out of
        Paradise. No one. Not
           even ourselves.

We did. We did besmirch
        the place. We shat on the floor
           of paradise.

We did. This is the truth. We did
        not get kicked out
           of Paradise. We turned

against paradise, the place we
        have always lived in.
           The only place we have

& which therefore has to be
        Paradise. We have
           no other, garden or

city, steppe or town. This here
        is Paradise. This
           now. We have shat on.

No one kicked us out. No one.
　　　　　Call him NoOne. NoOne
　　　　　　is to blame.

We shat all over the place.
　　　　　NoOne cleaned it up.
　　　　　　NoOne is to blame.

L'Heure Bleue
is the hour when the night
        birds have fallen
silent,
           & the birds
of day do not
yet stir

        a blue silence, night's oldest
        a blue hour, the coming day's youngest
hour, the
                not-yet-day's premonition, a per-
fume against the brain,
        the benjamin
of hours, smells of gum benzoïn, of *benjoïn*, gum
                Benjamin,

(not blue in itself,
            white or yellowish
                crystal compound

the name adrift as ever as they all are
            this one from Arabic
                luban jawi (frankincense from

        Java, from far into this night, into
        the blue of this hour, you are the oxygen
        of this blue hour

$C_{14}\,H_{12}\,O_2$

O two Oh you,
        Oxygen for two
                Blue hour of me and you

deturn Shri Jayadeva's hymn
        to Krishna's love making

"With Benjamin, the resin, trace

a sign on the perfect brows . . .
        Between her two breasts,
        cups of the firmament,
        the pearls of her necklace

invoke the zodiac."
        But the milky way
          Is drawn by
    Krishna's sap

in the blue hour
        he is the bee
           he eats her honey
                his torso thrown back

he says to her:
        "Come, trample my heart."
      (may they bring thus to an end
      the errors of this Kali Yuga!

Poem upon returning to these States
after a 6-months absence

yes, this is the Titanic
       yes, these are icebergs,
       no, upgrading to first class
       won't save your ass.

from *An Alif Baa*

preamble to an alphabet

letters arose
says Abu al-Abbas Ahmed al-Bhuni
letters arose
from the light of the pen
inscribed the Grand Destiny
on the Sacred Table

after wandering through the universe
the light transformed
into the letter *alif,*
source of all the others.

another arrangement of letters
into words & words
into stories has it
that Allah created the angels
according to the name & number
of the letters so that they should
glorify him with an infinite
recitation of themselves as arranged
in the words of the Qu'ran.

and the letters prostrated themselves
and the first to do so was the alif
for which Allah appointed the alif to be
the first letter of His name & of the
alphabet.

ا

[alif]

Adam is said to have written a number of books three centuries before his death. After the Flood each people discovered the Book that was destined for it. The legend describes a dialogue between the Prophet Muhammad and one of his followers, who asked: 'By what sign is a prophet distinguished?'

'By a revealed book,' replied the Prophet.

'O Prophet, what book was revealed to Adam?'

'A, b . . .' And the Prophet recited the alphabet.

'How many letters?'

'Twenty-nine letters.'

'But, oh Prophet, you have counted only twenty-eight.'

Muhammad grew angry and his eyes became red.

'O Prophet does this number include the letter alif *and the letter* lam*?'*

'Lam-alif is a single letter . . . he who shall not believe in the number of twenty-nine letters shall be cast into hell for all eternity.'

I.

and Alif has many seats
    under which he is silent
    though you cannot call it suffering
    suffering rhymes with zero
    at least initially
    a sweet round perfection
    as we like to draw it
    doodling one into the other

(newspaper margins of the b&w middle fifties
     at Mme Cavaiotti's where I wrote
     or learned to daily at 5 p.m. whose husband
     told me that in the last war (which wasn't
     the last at all) he had been
     forced to drink his piss from his boot
     in the desert of Libya, his wife linking
     zeroes, rounds, in the margins of the daily
     "*Wort*," making, making writing

a chain of nothingness
     that is something
     and that is our fate *und Fluch*:

     that we have to do something
          even to achieve the nothing
          even if only we doodle
          ourselves through life
          while talking on the phone
          to someone doodling elsewhere
          while all we mumble are
          sweet nothings chains
          of linked zeroes
                    yet
             step back &   focus shifts

          a shape emerges   from the space created

            by the two   circles'

              intersections,

        mandorla,
                wherein stands
        the shape of Celan's eye, of the fruit
    of the almond tree,
            there stood, maybe,
    the names of the six kings
    of Madyan, make up the letters
    of the Arabic
    alphabet.

        The nothing, where does it stand?
    It stands outside the almond,
    it stands in the shells
    of the suffer'un
    the zero-crescents
    above & below

("Human curl, you'll not turn gray,
        Empty almond, royal-blue")

fall away
        as the almond looms,
        yet remain as links
        of a chain,
        isthmus-claws
        sew mandorla to
        mandorla

2.

What a place that must be,
        a something at least, to be in
        and if that nothingness
        was the hamza

a sort of zag without a zig
a future breath half taken now
with always something more
solid, important coming right
behind it.
a kind of fishing hook.

which puts an odd occasion
on this table:
a fishing hook
equals
a future breath
here lie the roots of another
surrealism yet to come
when we find the zig goes with
the orphaned zag.

ب
[ba]

a homophone of house

where there is
a fishing hook
there is bait.
As big as a house
we can all live in.
the fish swim through it.
this is needed now
for the sun is going down
— maybe it was scared
by the cannon shot just hears

or maybe the cannon shot
was to announce the setting
of the sun.

It is strange
how cause & effect
can exchange places
as if this all was an old
old dance we are in
where without reason
we have to change partners.
I don't know. & don't
trust those who do
say they know.
& yet I am sure
of something: both cannon
sound & sun set
tell the same tale:
the people can break their fast
go into their houses
& find something to eat,
& should the larder be empty,
we can always eat the bait.

ن

A poem in noon

noon already
        yet dew
        persists
        in a letter
        framer of Enlightment

a vocalization of Arabic
& a discussion, no an
excerpt from a letter
— the other kind
or is it? —
in which Ghita
(a gain to open her name)
meditates on that most redolently
redundantly?
of poetic objects:
the dew drop —
        rosée
        dew
        nda

where our r, French,
        rolls & roils
        into the dark of a round
        wonder, a drop in
        a bucket, to re-emerge
        hissing wet, somewhat
        sheepish, but not *ain*
        so difficult to pronounce
        for northern *claritas*.
        Rosée, rosée you want to go on
        mad Brel sheep braying
        rosée, rosas, rosa, rosarum
        an elsewhere will have
        gobbled the drop by noon
        whereas dew dances
        on that soft initial d
        even if one suspect a

long gone missing hamza
that moment of separation
of drop & ether, air
the caught breath of
transformation
air into water
a condensation (a poem)
in itself.

we live on such false
      etymologies, on the real
      joy of sound-
      ing, it brings
      on what unravels
      in a word
      lip formed, throat instructed,
      scraping or not the roof
      of its tent,
      & way back of it,
      too high up to get
      that close
      or simply get it
      the brain amazed
      that shaped air
      makes sense
      in difference.
      Shut your brain port
      (as if, as if)
      for a moment
      open your mouth
      be wet sweet breath
      be dew

be dew
be the beduin
letter
be noon
be noon dew
between lips
be silk between
be between
the letter & the brain
the letter & the letter
be the hamza both
cuts & links,
be barzagh
be peninsula
be isthmus
be the moment between
   breathe, ride the breath
ride the separation between
   letter & letter
   the air bridge
   be there
   & listen:
rosée, dew — a due rose
triangulation with
soft sweet *nda*
hop over the bent back
of the initial, both hands
gently on that back
to gain air
becomes the slight
explosion of d
into that most initial & red

of vowels
arnica, all-healer
end of nda
but I err
the alphabet was wrong
the Arabic
noon
shaped
mirror reversal
over the horizon,
in its language
the letter a little
trough a gentle
curved cup
& the dew the drop
maybe is but the dot
hangs over it, thus:
ن

The Rheumy Eye of Night

thoughtthrobs castle the
        insomnia-scale
    bird beaks border the mater dura
    what can happen doesn't
    slow pain traces the hand bones
    the weak sunsmear easterns
       the horizon daily
          bleeds cold into onto
   char multiples ember into holes
   the horoscope of love falters
      the writer's hand crimps
         the accumulation of force
          shadows

& the voice says the speed of
      metaphor gets you
        nowhere fast

& the mast can't hold
     the thought of the sail
     in which the wind cringes
     in fear of its own consequences

carefree unsleep shudders
      a syntax of leaves
    the lacework of word after
      word harbors the peristalsis of time

shindig masters fart
       the *prophecylactics* of soul
       ghost ships down the Floridas
       of my & your blood
       what washes up on the see
       sure is a bottle or else
       the pro, the found, the con,
       the fuse of it all

there is no merit in furze
       the light turns yellow in between
       as sleep neither comes nor goes
       the extravagance of experience
       exhales exhausted into
       a null-community
       "sait la vie" no one whispers
       anything like it at the
       close of night, a rheumatics
       of soul.

Another end to writing/reading #18

           If
you cannot touch the
    untouchable,
        but you can look
where looking was forbidden.

    a shadowy suspicion
    an aroused content

disturbing to psyche
    but "Psyche was
a searcher in the story,
  as a consequence of her looking
    when looking is forbidden."   R.D., *The HD Book*

Look there, every-
    where   look at her.

    But we look to touch
and do so in the act
of looking —

    the desire of / in
the eye — fires
to hand to advance
    "he is looking to touch"

(touch assures being
ear /eye /nose assure well-being   J.D., *Le toucher*
    sez Aristotle

But the ear
　　　is the middle
　　　voice, in

one out the other
　　　side, tympanum
　　　or hymen

whatever plays either
　　　side, the skin mem-
　　　brane is

hide of an intelligence
　　　more telling than
　　　the core

so grey & massive
　　　a night in the ear
　　　in medina

the medully of tone
　　　is articulated affect
　　　pre-thought

in the middle of
　　　things, the double
　　　heard heart.

from PYRENEAN NOTEBOOK

✿ ✿ ✿

Along the coast of Sri Lanka fish feed
  on the corpses of the drowned

On the streets of Falluja dogs eat
  the bodies of the killed

In New Orleans there are corpses
  tethered to street signs & poles.

Trees, coral reefs & mangrove
  swamps are nature's shield.

"Poetry is something else. Heartgray, sublunar.
  Breathmarbled language in time."

The Sanctuary of Hands

1.

to cut beneath the humdrum
to get language on the road
to dig through the layers
from last night's hangover to
a Byzantine arch six hundred
years old, a carefully
constructed something, a
Ciceronian sentence, a habit
of daily diagnostics meant
to work language mano a mano
to breckel crumble it between
thumb & forefinger into
crumbs to feed the pigeons
& geese that press close in
the elaborate-starved gang-
ways of hunger-mind.

2.

mano a mano into the double
cave of Gargas
his fiction is of wild-he
& here the Commune of Aventignan,
is propriétaire & gestionnaire *of the mouth*
of that earhly swallowing-up.
Herein the long conduit

hands on walls
blown clear shadows against
stone all dated 27,000
years ago give or take
four centuries.

The countdown gives:
of 231 paintings of hands,
in negative outline & positive imprint, 114
show mutilations of one or more fingers,
only ten show no
deficiency in finger joints.
The remaining 107, not well enough preserved
through the millennia to allow a decision
as to whether they were mutilated or not.

There are right hands, there are left hands,
hand of women, hands of men, hands
of children

Note: all thumbs are there,
no thumb is mutilated,
oh opposable (self-)definition of the human,
these are

Cro-Magnon hands, fingers folded
in silent code as paint is blown
from mouth or bone to frame
a hand —
                    language of bent
fingers decodes the layers of
human understanding of
humans —

             if early is primitive, claims
mutilation in savage ritual Leroi-Gourhan's
theory wants to rhyme
finger mutilations with silent
hand code signals of
Kalahari Bushmen hunters'
info re presence of game:
Three folded middle fingers
spell "gazelle," the middle alone
"giraffe," an open
hand no fingers bent says
"monkey."

          or illiterate primitivism bias backed by
Catholic Church in Franco-cantabrian area
need therefore to insist on
          full linguistic & symbolic competence of palaeololithic humans

             if early is sickly, the claims
line up a delirious vademecum of modern medicine:
in the 1950ies, Paul A. Janssen championed Raynaud's disease
others ogled acute arthritis, syphilitic
arthritis, arteriosclerosis, embolism,
diabetic gangrene, obstructive thromboangiitis.
One Ali Sahly adds ainhum
(hereditary, but affecting only
the fifth finger & mainly known amongst male
Negroes in the tropics), leprosy (unlikely, because the metacarpals
do not seem
affected at Gargas), acrocyanosis,
and several afflictions such as chilblains &
rheumatism.

                    if early is rich culture birth read
                the missing fingers joints as folded in silent
                language code
        for writing is early

        though testing correlations for
                    recurring combinatorial patterns
                    remains to be done (find Hans Bornefeld's 1994
                    The Keys to the Caverns:
                    is very early & the archeology of
                    morning needs credit
                    Cro-magnon meander
                    which complicates mother
                    — nature or capital M,
                    goddess, black or white —

        & the shamaness knows the 'rooms
                    Clayton winds his way through
                    "In Gargas a quester writhed through, or ate mushrooms, or
                        fell asleep,   we will never know,
                    he turned himself into a uterine double,
                    he located the sole gate of access to paradise
                    he dived to the bottom of the sea,
                    followed a bear into a grotto, had the sense to listent o
                        a hedgehog,   we will forever know
                    the beautiful U-turn of his journey"

        he went in a boy
                    came out a girl

        woman, oh that
                    Olson's demand to Boldereff

"why don't you put this history together …
she's the CLUE, she, our SUMER GIRL!
(a hot idea,
should've been followed up in 1950

so that we could be done with
        the "hunting hypotheses"
        (there was no hunting in the caves,
        the hands the hands!

from THE FEZ JOURNALS

✿ ✿ ✿

Bab Bou Jeloud

Clouds today, at
              least a few
       to make the blue
              sky interesting.

What is green inside
              & blue outside?
       A gate named after
              a goat, its skin

at least like every true
              barrier or border
       it is more hole then wall,
              more to go through.

The moussem crowds moved
              me back & forth
       then kept me (moving) in the inside
              of the gate. A

gate is to walk through
              no matter the direction
       I was door, the crowd hinge
              I swung under its creak.

One could live there, I mean
              in the gate, be in shade
          but traversed by wind & people
              to live there & not be

a keeper — that is the challenge
              for under it the blue &
          the green become interchangeable
              for who lives there.

Only for those who come to it
              from either side will
          the colors matter, or at least tell them
              from where they are.

When you are the gate
              there is no need to know
          this subterfuge we call
              the inside & the outside

I am there again, favorite place
              is middle, isthmus
          the between: the only place that is
              all we can be in at once.

In Larache

I.

When colonialism holds you — French
        there, Spanish here — an old
        architecture circles the plaza,
        crenellating the minds.

The two young women
        we stay with
        speak perfect Spanish
        for having gone to Spanish
        school here in Larache
        since age 3. Cannot read
        a street sign in Arabic,
        their language.

2.

        this time it is here:
        the lead of religion.
        it is all over

it is all over
        when in the beginning is
        perfection

it is all over
        when the only hankering

is for pristine Medina
it is all over
when the educated middle class
techno-savvy as any *roumi*

says there is no veil
over the book, only
over the woman.

3.

a mint tea on the plaza
& now another on el balcon
atlantico facing
that western ocean
a pressed orange
on the horizon
in my glass
& a black coffee,
aaah! happiness at 8 a.m.

4.

in the Maghreb of the Maghreb
on the farthest western point
there where the desert army
is stopped
by the sea
where Sidi Okhba
danced his horse prancing into
the waves,
where now the mosque of

Hassan II sits on land
stolen from the people,
there spins the mad dervish of
the Maghreb, spins &
spins — it is no longer
a dance, there is no ecstasy
to it, only pain & breath-
lessness — he spins
& spins & doesn't know
in which direction to stop,
east toward Mecca
west toward America
he twists & twists
skewered by
Ameccarica
the nightmare
from which there is
no waking up.

5.

Here lies
     ci-gît
     Jean
     Genet,

brought back
     to Larache
     in a burlap sack
     tagged
     "immigrant worker,"

now

>two white stones
>at head & foot
>green plants
>in between

looks out

>over Ocean —
>tired from
>a long death:

the stone says

>he was born
>as we all are
>on one day

but he died

>on both the 14
>and 15 April.

What if the birds were the shadows
       & the shadows on the earth the letters?
       There is an earthling's logic
       to this proposition, even if
       not that of the breakfast just had.

That one leaves no shadow:
       what goes in is dark matter
       what goes out is dark matter
       in between some light happens
       & energy is shadowless we know

except we know Hiroshima too,
       or do we? A busload of Japanese
       women at breakfast this Fez morning
       an odd way to break into
       an egg, hard-boiled, with a spoon

hammering rings of Saturn around
       the ovoid's middle. Why is there no
       small mushroom cloud shaped
       like a shadda for emphasis above
       their heads? We go about our

business — & holidays is the busiest
       business — as if there was no history,
       no yesterday — only a tomorrow
       and that one perilously shaped like
       today. The waiter clears the table.

Outside the little red taxis warm
        themselves — or each other? — in the
        rising sun. An unborn species
        of animal, a moving thing-animal
        from the other side of the sea, being

washed by its drivers, lovingly
        drenched with what gives us all life.
        As if it were those watery ablutions
        made them run, not the
        refined matter of dispute in earth's depth.

We look out, all of us, the shaddas
        over out heads lift, as our images
        split in two by night come back
        together, a semi-solid ovoid daydream
        around our square breakfast tables.

CANTO DIURNO #5

Paris, 22 August 2006

✼ ✼ ✼

1. At the Mondrian

(11.30 a.m.
w/ fake real coffee from Papua
New Guinea — does that make the espresso pod
feral? — or just fruity & balanced as advertised?
stiff back against striped plush, unbendable,
the start of something,
a form, the woman
in the red car at the traffic light
shifts & drops her cell phone —
the *camionette* with the sad-faced
Mediterranean driver — a Lebanese
pastry delivery van, the cedar
on the door looks forlorn,
its left branch peels off,
drips to street level
I want to wave
hesitate as to how
a smile? a shrug of the shoulder,
fatalistic? encouraging?
a thumb's up? a fist raised
quickly pumped a yes, yes?
light changes, van
moves on, driver's expression
unchanged, I remain en-

> tangled in my
> choices, unable to pick, sign
> language, I realize, not any
> easier then words then try to
> relay this moment
> it took 10 minutes to write
> down.

& yet:

> To respond to any figure
> of outside so much more difficult
> than to write down what comes in
> > to eye from out
> there as say Brainard or Pérec did
> > (neither they nor I sit much in the *Café*
> *de la Mairie* these days
> where Pérec listed his eye's world)

> another van with smiling
> Maghrebian driver parks right
> there: sanitary installation,
> work, fixing up the fine French
> building on the boulevard St Germain,
> untouched by the bombs falling
> on buildings in Beirut in
> the mind of the Lebanese pastry
> delivery man.
> > (young man on roller blades falls
> down right in front of the
> parked van, gets up smiling,
> no bullet has eaten his liver,
> protected as he is by a fake American
> tee-shirt, wipes hands

on jeans, skates on.
      (just across from the Mondrian
the old Polish bookshop appears
between a bus & a truck, spiffed up
now — a sign of the times, most
books now in French & English
translations among well-printed Polish editions
: should I go over & ask
for a complete works of Joseph
Conrad in Polish. Does it exist?
Has JC been returned from his exile?

No one returns from exile. In
      hajara there are no u-turns
      for you or any one,
      only the aaa's of surprise or
      pain, only
      always the beginning of
      the alphabet.
      exile is always beginning
      anew,
      exile is the sun rising each
      morning, & realizing
      (not the sun, who knows or
      doesn't care, no you) you
      realizing that this is the first
      day, again & again,
      the first day, the
      unknown, each morning
      you have to find, as you
      start again, the
      ahh of surprise
      on the breath.

2. Lunch at La Grille (1:30 p.m.)

a
calf's
head
sauce gribiche
pour it on
a childhood pleasure
the creamy white brain
a nano *haut-le-coeur*
(heart rises to brain to speak its mind)
at the circumvolutions (? check
dictionary — months of French
overlay English – instability of
vocabulary — shimmy back & forth —
love your false friends — words
migrate in all seasons — as word
for all reasons? — spice up your
vagrant vocables — *scheinheilige* —
where does that German word
come from, now, here, at la Grille,
the grille, the lattice work, whispered
through the monkish grate at
back of mind by childhood
prompter, or Celan's speech-grille?
((*Eisheiliger, Eisbein, Eiswein*
or is it the ¼, un quart
Pouilly-Fuissé speaking (*schein-
heilig*)
        sheen-holy,

the brain, the brain = a childhood taste
        on toast with black

butter & capers, fork-mashed mother's treat
— or medical school shiver, cut
-ting into soft tissue, an organ
(ogre) held in — fitting, filling —
both hands, shaky pudding
thumbs on "foramina" (*sulcus*
is that the word, *sulcus terminalis,*
a furrow twice explored – slight shiver
helps knife — as if it needed it —
slice through non-resistant tissue,
careful/careless share — to eat
everything (a pig, well-used
is 450 servings snout to tail
a pig is *haram* in Beirut & Darfur,
I am ashamed as I shiver
through the brain — the one on the
plate, or the one in it's case, this skull? —
a shiv, romantic twitch
in an imagined *zigeuner* underground
the blubbery cheek — black skin
(Miles called it green on the
pintade's armpit, refused to
eat, a shudder bigger, more
intractable than my shiver —
shudder of the unknown as
against shiver of history (personal
repetition) easily overcome by
mouth pleasure, tongue in slomo
crushes soft slice against top of
the mouth, palate palace
roof & last sip.
lean back.

Blurb for Hütte

The building of thought

The making of thought dwells in
     the building it is in

[building — dwelling — thinking

a questioning of the provincialism *revendiqué* by H.
     a demythologizing
     a gainst "grim fascination" with the hut

Here's a backdoor way —
     revealing, modest, straight —
     into Heidegger's Hütte, from the
     ground plan. to the higher
     reaches of the philosopher's
     thought,

The importance of the place,
     qua physical locale, where
     thinking — even the most abstract
     thought — happens cannot be
     underestimated.

another keep
     that keeps the world at critical distance
     from H — this is no fawning *laudatio*

Reading Edmond Jabès

Here, the end of the word, of the book, of chance.

Desert!
> Drop that dice. It is useless.

Here, the end of the game, of resemblance.
> The infinite, by the interpretation of its letters
> Denies the end.

Here, the end cannot be denied. It is infinite.

Here is not the place
> Nor even the trace.

Here is sand.

I like the imp
      in impossibility
      that makes it all
      possible

Homage to Badia Masabni

shift & tell
  a rhythm travelled
  along the silk
  road from central
  Asia going West
  gone South
  shifte telli
  ah! Madame Masabni
  you added violins,
  cellos, accordions & ouds
  to the traditional line-up
  of riqq, derboukka, ney or zurna —

& the girls, the girls
  now shift across the silk stage
  & their tell-tale arms
  move the story along
  snake arms & veils
  (probably seen in Isadora's
  Paris shows)
  and the belly was
  now only one mooring,
  moving part
    from East to
  West & back
  shivering
   the spine of the
  Urals.

from THE BOOK OF U

Two for the Cormorants

1.

the heart of
the cormorant

is at the head
of its name

it wants more
but no rant

2.

we applaud
the cormorant

even if the fish
slipping down

its gullet
won't.

In the dog days of summer, 3 of 'em:

1.

Thinking,
        in Europe
        begins,
        suggests Pascal
        Quignard, that is,
        in *Mourir de penser*
        with Argos,
        Odysseus' dog
        cf. Od. XVII, 301
            Enosèn Odyssea eggus eonta
        translates literally as
        he *thought "Odysseus" in him*
                who moved toward him.

2.

Which makes me think
        on lines by Habib Tengour
        I translated a dog's age ago
        & which read:

"Homer will say that nobody recognized him — Ulysses —, except the old dog. But dogs don't live long enough to recognize their masters."

3.

& riding the subway, this morning,
          this:

a (baseball) cap   on the N train

                    In dog years
                    I'm dead

in red
          on pink cap
          of a very alive
          Indian lady in her
          thirties.

After Basho

A bird a pleasure to see
though soon, sadness:
boats yes, but no cormorant.

又たぐひながらの川の鮎なます

omoshirote /yagate kanashiki /ubune kana
oh mush I wrote / vacate can as hickey / you bun a can a

summer's so

> shortsighted while
> in winter through
> bare branches
> I see the ships
> lying in wait
> along the length
> of the Narrows
> & the gulls eyeing
> their sterns
> waiting for garbage —

my cormorants

> don't go there
> (that's a statement,
> not an order
> there's no ring around
> your neck
> > in either, in
> any season.

The one & only

cormorant was waiting
right there
at the elbow
the 69th street pier &
the Narrows walkway made.
Sitting some ten feet off-
shore, neck craning, eye taking
it all in,
       sea & land,
I wondered if . . .
or started to
but it dove for breakfast as
I picked up walking speed
earphones broadcasting
France Cul interview
with Jacques Rancière
by Laure Adler,
the theme "It is not
democracy that's exhausting itself,
but oligarchy," while
I looked back twice
— not over French Marxist thinking
but over the undisturbed surface
of the Narrows,
           then moving
forward into speed-walking

hip swinging mode
I'm overtaken
50 feet to my right
by said bird —
the cormorant, not Rancière —
doing its quiet cormorant
best
　　flying south just above
the surface, skimming ahead
as I pick up speed
now see it at the level of
the 86th street flyover
settled again & diving
as I come up to it
it breaks surface,
silvery fish at a 90° angle
in beak, as if showing off
the twitching freshness of the
catch, down its gullet it goes,
　　as I hear Jacques Rancière
explain the need back when,
I know not, missed that bit, but
long before I had ever met
a cormorant, the need to think with
Debray — whom I had met &
who had swallowed me
like the cormorant its fish —
the notion of a revolution
in the revolution,
to create that living space *in*
between — as I would put it
now — a lagoon

betwixt the gulag of totali-
tarianism & the gulag of
capitalism.
          That was the only
what's his name, my bird,
black lightning without thunder,
my poorer memory at seventy,
my cormorant, the only
such cormorant this morning,
made my morning in the
sweltering anthropo-
scene called
New York.

Last cor poem

walking my
       walk along the
       Narr-
       ows

a mile
       a mile & a half
       2 miles

turning back
       turning a-
       round all
       that's left
       are

Paul's gulls

not even Nicou's
       ducks, what
       are they?

called? hooded
       Mergansers I
       think,
       though that sounds like

Meer
Gans to me, sea goose
what do I know, call them
Lophodytes cucullatus
what do I know, only
words,
can't tell the ani-
mal, the
ani-
ma,
lazy mammal I
am walking the
walk skirting my
own narrows

where there are
neither gulls
nor ducks

& it seams like
I mean seems
like in looks like

the only
cormorant
the only one
of my birds
left

is me

& I worry
that I may be

more rant
        than
        core.

from FOX-TRAILS, -TALES & -TROTS

A Poem in Luxembourgish on New York

Because to speak, to speak like one's mother, means to dwell,
even there where there are no tents.
— Paul Celan (translated here by the author)

It wasn't even around Pentecost
    and nothing was flowering
    but it was an overheated day
    mid-February & mid-town
    when twixt Anselm Kiefer at the Breuer-Met
    & Wagner's Parsifal at the Met-Opera
    I sat down in the middle of Central Park
    on a bench exactly twixt those two Euro-Kulchural affairs
    to write this poem.

(Don't buy that hotdog, nor any of those
    nuts, too much sugar in both, but)
    look
    at that white horse, that nag
    makes no mistakes.
    it eats its oats
    and works through this heat,
    head bowed, gemütlich
    it shows New York
    to the tourists much better
    than I could.

And the horse is neither sad-sack nor amused, like any
    thing or person pulling some form of transport
    conundrum through New York,

it or he or she's smilingly sullen
or sullenly smiling & about ready to nap.

I nod to the nag which doesn't
        nod back, busy as it is to rhythmically
        nod its head following its heavy trot.

And I keep nodding, body/mind
        caught in rhythm of horse's
        nod, the clop-clop of its hoofs
        and, a hundred meters to the right,
        the quick nervous bang-bang of jazz drums

it's all one
    ·   gorgeous
        rhythmic mess,
                it is the beat-
        ing heart of New York, & thus the true
            heartbeat of
        America —
                even if I am —
        no, not caught, but — strolling, or
        sitting in the sun
        between two Euro-references,
        but in the middle of the heat of this city
        I fell
        in love with exactly fifty years
        & seven moths ago
        even if not always faithful —

                — & now I need
        a table & a cup-a-coffee — a question: the waitress'
        head raises — "straight up"

I say —
then sit down
    right in the window of the
European Café
        (a name & a place
        does not translate into
            Café Europe my old hangout on the Plëss)
there where
Columbus & Broadway
intersect &
now bring
this poem to
a close.

Letter to Steichen's Ed

*In fact, every photograph is a fake from start to finish, a purely impersonal,
unmanipulated photograph being practically impossible.*
— Edward Steichen

Leiwen Ed,

Ech wees net ops du ons Sproch nach gekannt hues,
       that's why I'll address you in American English.

You were born zu Béiwen, bei Roeser, in Luxembourg,
       I was not
       You were an American citizen,
       I am still not,
       I am just a plain citizen of Luxembourg.

You believed in the family of man
       I am weary of families of any order & species.

But you *are* family
       in that photo by Dana those clear blue
       Luxembourg eyes exactly like cousin Lol's, the cut
       of the face too, there's a resemblance, close to
       the bone, close to the farm
       a way in which the head
       is held. High & loose. You're my home-
       boy of old, Ed, a
       cousin, maybe even
       "cousin germain"
       as the French wld say?

Now, you burned your paintings
  when your gardener imitated one of yours —
  a strange act, a criticism of
  the representation of representation, maybe?
  Or just a cheap trick to prove Duchamp wrong
  for saying "stupide comme un peintre"
  & move on to the new technologies?

Now, I never burned a single poem
  have kept them all,
  but then you had Carl Sandburg
  in the family, devoted companion
  for long walks & writing for you

I have always hated taking
  photos but bought a camera at sixty
  to shoot landscapes
  & the family of one Joris
  & half a dozen friends
  but I always leave it home
  or forget that it is in my pocket.

You were a famous delphinium breeder
  I only brood over words
  make poems & make anthologies,
  weird cut flower bouquets

I am in Albany NY & sometimes
  visit Buffalo where
  you did avant-garde color autochromes
  the year Ford introduced the model T-Ford
  and one year after Picasso painted
  his *Demoiselles.*

Ah the autochrome!
>Hot off the 1903 minds
>of the Frères Lumière,
>them I've seen the Light Brothers,
>first marketed in our year 1907,
>it is an additive method
>a process involving millions
>of microscopic
>grains of potato starch
>(did you ever think of
>the Luxembourg staple
>food, *d'gromper*, when you
>loaded the camera?)
>dyed
>bright blue-violet,
>bright orange-red
>& Kelly green
>dusted on a slightly concave piece of glass
>already coated with liquid pitch mixed
>with a dram of beeswax
>to keep it "tacky"
>the random spaces filled with lamp-black
>& a panchromatic silver halide emulsion

the resultant screen
>was stochastic in nature
>a random array
>an abstraction way beyond the *Demoiselles'*
>demure cubism
>though the light you let
>pass through the photo-sensitive plate
>coming off
>your "subjects," say Charlotte

Spaulding in Buffalo,
with the starch grains remaining as aligned
as the starch of her lacy dress
organized this randomness into
plain Edwardian beauty.

Ed, you were not Edwardian,
you were just a Luxembourg lad
in America who made good
& moved with ease between
Condé Nast & this here place,
fifty years before Warhol.

If I am trying so hard to
understand this autochrome process
(of which you said "no medium
can give me color of such
wonderful luminosity")
it is because you also said:

"If you don't take doors off their hinges,
how are you going to know
to put doors back on their hinges?"

Though that, cousin Ed,
may be where we disagree:
why put the doors back on
the hinges,
beauty will bolt anyway,
and all we are ever left with
is the beauty of doing the work,
the handwork, the hands on work,
your plates, my words.

Merci, cousin,

  'daz gut ze wessen
  daz du hei wars virun mir.

from INTERGLACIAL NARROWS

from *LŒSS & FOUND*

✿ ✿ ✿

Elegy for Anselm Hollo

1.

eyes

   eyes
   eyes

invisible the eyes

a thousand
   crows
   on the snow

& yet, 2 crows
   already make a crowd

2.

& yet,
   we have to travel, Anselm
   because there are wines
   that don't.

3.

Ich trinke aus zwei Gläsern
 as we both
 zackern
 at the royal caesura
 the wandering eyes
 in the crow's nest
 between poem & translation
 translation & poem

bringing it all
 back home.

Avicenna to Break Up

Avicenna: sometimes singular beings
beings singular sometimes : Avicenna

among the humans
sromuoh eht kcoma

emigrate   there. It is a start we cannot
        cannot
      we start fr-

      -om, is it there
or dissociate from the journey. We may

     separate,
  part.   or
    secede

                    the first stem
        cuts off from friendly association

                single flower in cut
                crystal vase
            rose of Ibn "'Arabi" yet

                foe sore, read, dear
                    backwards
                    a sore foe
            even if raw war draw
            soar rose out of cow
            shed first appearance
                rewrite as

        Men must not be the maintainers of women
                because Allah has made some
            because they spend out of their property;
        the good women are therefore not obedient,
                    guarding the unseen
                those on whose part you fear
                        desertion,
                admonish yourselves, & leave
                    them alone don't
        beat them; do not seek a way against them;
                surely Allah is High.

                Avoid association with
                    or don't. the
                second stem. there is often
            explicit or implicit reference
                a sexual relationship

the third stem

a mutual ending of friendly relation,   the third stem

thus not flight properly but
the breaking of the ties of kinship
thus met thirst

Induce someone to
emigrate
send her to the desert,
Hagar

.

A bowshot away,
Be'er-Sheva or the valley of Makkah.
A skin of water then thirst.
Under a bush, heel
scratches a well into the desert.
Zamzam
Breakup
Emigrate   /   immigrate
the different sides of
the same coin. Koiné.
Porous borders.

Sudanese Saying

One of the non-
bourgeois of Calais
on one of the last days
of the Great Emptying
I.E. the Shameless Hiding
of the "eyesore"
Calais refugee camps
called "the jungle"
where "jungle" is a translation
of Pashto "dzhangal"
meaning "forest,"
one of these non-
bourgeois of Calais
reported
a Sudanese saying
to object to their,
the refugees' dispersal,
a saying that says
solidarity
alleviates pain,
& this is how
it goes:
"if we die all together,
death is a feast."

Marasma redirects

    to *Cnaphalocrocis* which eventually
    lands me on the genus
    medinalis, the rice leaf roller
    a species of moth of
    the *Crambidae* family
    found in south-east Asia,
    if you want to know more check
    Wikipedia I'm sending you there
    as I have to go out now
    to make sure the blue
    of the sky is still holding
    up those beech trees, & the
    others whose names I don't
    know & who may therefore
    be standing up on their own
    or possibly under different names
    as it is only what we can name
    that we can knock down
    why do you think those people
    painted all those animals
    in the caves of prehistory —
    it was a school, not a pit
    or shaft, & the little ones
    didn't giggle (as ours would)
    pointing to the dots naming
    the rhino turds but all to-
    gether in their languages made up

— that is, intoned —
the names of the living
creatures we call lion, bison, bear,
shaman, & have
not only named but
called so often & killed
when they came now
nothing or nearly nothing
left & the children
of our children will have to
relearn the names of the stones
or whatever else may be left.

our unconscious is always
        domiciled somewhere
says Gaston Bachelard

Yes, says I, it's always
        right there
           in
    our bodies.

Haiku for the End of the World

gaia world
sapiens not so sapiens
boom kaboom

The Poet's Job

pick up everything that shines
discard the gold

keep the light

Triggernometry of the Trinity

And the Lord, having rested from his labors, sat up, looked around &
seeing how His critters had fucked up His creation, He raised his hand &
put a bullet through his head.

Thus the Third Eye came to be.

A Late Antler for Dawn Clements

It may rise
        from the lowest left
        corner's edge,
        it may arch gracefully
        across space
        & does
        it may come down again
        at the other end
        heavy with accumulated
        matter
                bone & pearl,
        but it never will
        disappear again,
        it is there,
        in mid-air,
        it is ready
        & transforms
        into branch
        on tree,
                it now
        holds the bird-
        woodpecker or bluejay?
        -form you have moved
        into,
                just beyond

the double flame
one real
        the other
real too, a real
        image of you in
congress with
matter, mater
of us all.
        The antler,
the antler!
        you gave
me in celebration of
birth,
        is no hunter's death trophy
is your creation, a making
not ex nihilo,
        but ex, but out of
love,
        it is there,
I am with it, counting
        the pearls.

The Art of the Fugue, no,
not today, this
morning it is
    L'art de la fugue,
or how to run
    away from yourself
to come
    to yourself
through an outside
— snow this morning —

that lives up to
& beyond your vague
ideas of any other
beyond —

— a behind, rather, as from
the other side of this page
the ink bleeds through,
my contra-fugue,
     that goes into
         das geht in die Fugen,
an in-between
         daß es kracht
my counter-move & -sound,
         mirror image(s)
      brings nothing home, except
right now what stops
my Sturm, this metaphor:
      that ink can bleed or
can it?

Purgatory is
      forever,
  because
the barzakh is all
there is,

paradise & hell
but momentary
passages,
     the holes
in fact, that fit

the sprockets
of the daily
in *Fege-*
feuer's link
chains.

Shipping Out at 1:25 p.m. on Herman Melville's 200 birthday

HEAVENS GATE is headed for Whitehall at 16.7 knots

ATLANTIS is headed for NY Harbor at 8.4 knots

OWLS HEAD is headed to New York NY at 22.8 knots

ATLANTIC COMPASS is heading for USNYC at 15.5 knots

SPIRIT OF AMERICA is headed more or less toward Staten Island at
    16.9 knots

THEN AGAIN is headed nowhere at 4.4 knots

THOMAS JEFFERSON rests at Weehawkin NJ Pier 79 at 0.2 knots

ANTHEM OF THE SEA heads toward Kings Wharf, Bermuda at 0
    knots

JEWEL OF THE HARBOR is hiding under the Verrazano-Narrows
    bridge

SPIRIT OF NEW JERSEY is headed to Town Point Park at 7 knots

PARADIGM is heading somewhere at 8.3 knots, visible from my
    window

HENRY HUDSON is doing a Harbor Cruise at 4.2 knots

ELANDRA CORELLO AND NANCY P rest near Constable Hook

CELESTIAL is heading north at 5.5 knots

MEMORIES MADE lies at 0 knots in Edgewater

DANA ALEXA is headed for Bay Ridge Flats at 1.6 knots

BW RHINE is headed for NL RTM at 0.4 knots

RADIANT PRIDE is headed nowhere at 0.0 knots

DESTINY was traveling at 6.2 knots to an unknown destination 10
    minutes ago

A three-minute composition à la mode Dalachinsky to celebrate Steve

And when I crossed
      the street — Saint Marks'
        it was
from Porto Rico Imports
      to the North East Corner
        of 2nd & St. Marks
I thought I should
      go sit on the terrace
        of the Dallas Barbecue
to write this poem to
      you, Stevo, to
        celebrate your days & nights
in New York, as New York, as in-
      carnation, as New York
        is incarnation or you
are incarnation of
      to celebrate your days
        & nights that is
your life here
      as I remember an occasion when
        I crossed this street
Saint Marks where by all rights
      I shoulda have run
        into you back
when — 69, 70, 71? —
      but didn't or we did

                but didn't know
who we were
                too stoned maybe
                to look out
stuck inside not only the Big Shitty
                but our own young selves
                selvas oscuras
if you permit me
                to quote that obscure
                        Eye-talian, Dante
in the East Village psycho-deli-
                catessen's jungle-under-
                        -growth & -ground
& right here I was again am again
                coming from
                Porto Rico
Imports with my twice
                1 & a half pound
                        coffee beans under-
arm & crossing over to the
                North-East corner of 2nd & St Marks
                        on a late summer early evening
& didn't think of
                going to sit down on the Dallas BBQ
                        terrace because for the nth time I
wondered what the fuck a Texican BBQ
                was doing in the
                East Village
on that hallowed corner
                just across Gem
                        Spa's where back when
when "when" was now we'd run into Ginsie
                picking up his just delivered

copy of tomorrow's *New York Times*
& anyway that time the terrace
was clearly full no place
for me, every chair
taken & on two of them
around a small table laden
with food
there you & Yuko sat absorbed
& digging in with
visible pleasure
though neither sun nor hunger nor napkin
could wipe away that
slight smirk of skepticism
played around your mouth
from birth — you hadn't seen me yet
so I took out my phone
shifted coffee bags under left arm
& snapped you & Yuko eating
(see, here is the photo
I'm not making this up, then you saw
& said Hi Bub,
& I said Stevo
Jolli-O,
got to boogie
to a reading
you said go man go
say hello to the lady
maybe I'll see you later
have two other
gigs I need
to catch first
And when I crossed that
street again in the first

            line of this poem,
my friend, it was cold
            & wintery & all the tables
                & chairs were empty
I thought of sitting down
            to write this poem
                but there was no music
to cut the cold
            & so I moseyed on
                til nights later I mean
like tonight, it came kinda natural
            took out pen & notebook
                just as Joëlle & Fay
started to play here at
            the Zürcher, with Yuko
                a few chairs away
& Nicole sketching
            in the back & you
                not kwetsching by my side
but here, yes, here,
            here to hear
                hear to be here, that
music, here
            lend me your ear
                Stevo, Stevo,
Dala, Dala, Mensch I miss
            you
                so.

from **HOMAGE TO CELAN**

✡ ✡ ✡

Earlier today I saw
  an old atlas
  floating down
  the Verrazano Narrows.

Which had nothing
  or something
  to do with my surprise,
  later today, seeing a
  footnote
  defined Celan as
  "translator and poet Paul Celan"
  (Rankine, Claudia
    Don't let me be lonely)
  & goes on:
  "committed suicide in 1970"

floating down
  the Seine,

for so many years,
  my Atlas.

A Poem or something, a gift, a song,
for Paul Celan at 100

Her hand giant shadow
    — *mit Bleistift*
on ceiling with night
reading light
pillowed between us —
graphites an unseen
page, on which
I'll write, standing up
in the kitchen,
                the good, no
the best thing about
night is it is
always a pre-
dawn.
           It goes way back,
1/2 time between your birth
& now, I
with a double breath-
turn (yours & mine),
embarked —
    before take-off
        father had asked for
           a shakehand
(a poem is that
    you said and
then let go)   in
              not my mother-
                tongue

                    in my future
            language he knew but reversed
        from early 1945 camp
            fires in another night,
a
darker one you
knew too.
            What had freed father,
            drew me over,
            (you already knew better
            had — August '49 — heard
            Gordon Heath sing climbing
            jacob's ladder, "twice he sang it, at
            the beginning and at the end"
            & in between strange fruit
            & a fraught encounter with
            the blond Northerner still &
            always freed fascist "doing Paris"
            at your table in, not on, the échelle)

and we are climbing some kind of ladder
        different for each as should be
            you to Paris
                me to New York
                    both with faith only in no faith
        the right to blaspheme
        as first right left
            after the third reich fell then
            & now the first empire here
        is falling down
falling down.
            My first crossing

(between your visit to Heidegger
          & your first trip to Berlin)
    ferried me across the Charlie Gibbs
          fracture zone a transform fault dis-
              places the Mid-Atlantic Ridge,
lands me in a "thickness:
    to be understood from the geological,
          and thus from the slow
              catastrophes & the dreadful fault-
    lines of language — —"
          but it is there
in the faultlines that writing starts. You wrote:
    "Columbus,
    eyeing the autumn-
    colchis, the mother-
          flower,
              murdered masts & sails. Everything set forth,
    free," (but we ban
that late loser, found
& lost
          by people he murdered,
another, our, atonement, I, here still
fifty years after your death —
which is not that of the book, that buch-,
that buch-
stable staff as
the beech is as the tree is the book the Buche
from your Book
-ovina, the
    first book, the one that
has the autumn crocus
only only a secret echo

of the literally timeless,
name of their *colchique,*
our autumn crocus
called up by reality
to meet again in the imagination
of your city, my city
all gathered in
one stands brightly on no
hill but by the sea, even if a black
sea, even if Colchis
is & is not
New York
from where I greet you
this morning
on your hundredth birth
day.

from *UP TO & INCLUDING THE VIRUS:*
DIARETICS 2020–2021

✿ ✿ ✿

1/30

It is still night,
      the words as yet as few
      as there are lights
      on the opposite shore

All shores are opposite
      — but opposite what?

My eyes, no — they have to be in
      my eyes for me to see,
      they are opposite the night
      and touch, the lights
      are the night.

1/31

The great dying of the birds
      puts cheap gas into your cars
      & a feather on the hat
      of this & that
      "industry," celebrating
      its adage, a dollar is
      worth more than a life,
      any life.

Note to Self on 11 February

cell-sense   (N)
     cell-self   (P)

the body politic of the
     community of one's cells —
     as place of reflection:

the cell & its relation to sugar —
     N's contention that it, the cell,
     will go for the easiest high, &
     loves sugar — & by mimesis (? —
     my word here) we, that organized bag
     of cells do the same.
          I.E. life's like that, or that's life
     goes for
     the quick fix —

          & the birds love the fermented berries,
          getting loaded's a treat
            for them too!

monday feb 24, 6:30 a.m.

EST time on
NY–AbuDhabi flight
(5 hours sleep, wow: long ago in
dream we
crossed the Charlie Gibbs
fracture zone the transform fault
displaces the Mid-Atlantic Ridge,
but now awake ahead as
on the map
we have just crossed
the Tigris
& the language
rightly so
veers to Arabic
again & again
no matter how often
or hard I hit
the English button,
but refreshes too
quickly for my rusty
decipherment of
that Alif baa to
give me the info
I want
the plane now halfway
over Basra

halfway over
the Gulf, history
old & new
rushes in.

*

A Shelter Is Not Necessarily An Island
as title for something cogent right now
comes to mind & brings to mind
Eric Mottram's 1971 book title
   Shelter Island & The Remaining World
    so now is shelter
the opposite of the
    "remaining world"
— when the remaining world is
helter-skelter (late 16th century adverb: a rhyming jingle of unknown
  origin,
perhaps symbolic of running feet or from
Middle English *skelte* 'hasten') —
    or not? No,
shelter is island
    island is always plural
is always already part of
     some
multiplicity, an archipelago
"a series of sound groups   a local thrush
    chickadees at their red plastic spinning bins
     active for dark brown striped white
sunflower seeds
gull's white crab and cree low over wrinkling shore planes"
     (E.M., *Shelter Island*)

3/24

Outside:
                sun caught
        in bare tree branches,
                      cradled

Inside:
                me caught
        in shelter in place,
                      cradled too

p.s. We shall both
                rise again

3/30

Thinking of a possible essay on "commissure" that piece, that place conjoining Celan & Olson, I just came across this in an old notebook, 8 June 1971, London, a day on which I threw the I Ching & got:

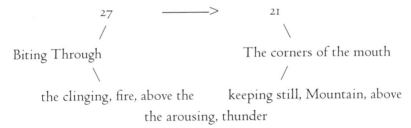

3/31

We are only eternal while we are alive.

4/1

These buds on the branches
        here this year too
        their steadfastness . my surprise

*

Nachhaltige Nicht-Nachhaltigkeit
        = title of a German book
        translates as:
                sustainable non-sustainability
        (or: the empire strikes back . . .)

4/5

    All morning into early afternoon preoccupied with the dead per-
    son found under the pine-tree in the Narrows Botanical Garden
    right across the street under our windows.

Young guy
in our building found the corpse — we had been wondering
as we saw police huddled, delimiting the area with yellow tape,
if it was a vagrant, possibly sick with Covid-19, an overdose,
or what else. I did think for a brief moment that it could be a
suicide. Later a black NYC van stopped, left again, returned.
The coroner, no doubt. The body, covered by a white sheet or
body-bag was all the more visible — for hours. The young
man who found him confirmed (talking to Nicole window to
sidewalk) that it was a suicide, most likely, middle-aged white
male, not a vagrant, well-dressed, strange manner of death,
I.E. hanging himself from a very low branch, body prone on
ground. Possible murder? Execution? Can't find anything yet
in the local news. Nicole lit a candle, as we wished him good
travels through the barzakh.

✻

During a zoom reading by Jerome Rothenberg
Two thousand run
    of the mill Buddhas
    tread water

There are no mirrors
    anywhere in the world
    : only others

In several parts
    the whole
    is & is not

The whole is
       & is not
       in separate parts

In acts of cruelty
       the present is miscarried
       again & again

Time you say is a bullfight
       I say time is kneeling
       in the sand hour before the bull

4/12

So in the last dream,
Derrida comes down the
majestic red-carpeted
staircase just before day
breaks & with a
large smile & an even
more expansive wave
of his left arm
(the other rests on the
baluster) gives the
order for the gerrymandering
to begin or to end
I can't be sure how
this one links to the
long black & white
dream just before (only
a quick pee separates

them) in which I talked
lengthily to various politicians
and a few pundits
(me included, it seems)
about the evil of
gerrymandering, &
we are all absolutely
certain, as certain as one can
only be in a dream, that
our lives depend on
ending that terrifying
trend & now that I
woke up for good I
would really like to go
back into the last one
and ask Jacques if his
gesture meant to begin
or to end what the
dream proposed. But I
can't, I can't, the sun
has risen behind me
where I can't
see it though
I do see its reflection right
in front of me, reddening
the East Coast buildup
West of here & on
of Staten Island just
across the Verrazano Straights
much more quiet today
these waters, not half as roiled
as yesterday or as my dreams
made me today.

4/14

So what is there left
        except for the light
        of a watery sun slanting
        through clouds,

some cars, some runners
        all wearing masks except
        for those three in a circle
        (what is a circle of three?)

(((there is
        no way of
        squaring that one
        except as the four-line
        stanza, come in without asking
        & now broken up))

based on 6 feet distance
        who are smoking in concert
        and that 5-kid family of
        orthodox Jews rushing toward

the pier & maybe the water
        will part & they can
        escape the plagues of New York
        — no pharaoh will chase them to no paradise.

from 5/22

We always say
       he or she died —,
       that can be 700 years
       ago in the
       past or today in what we call
       the present, though not that tense,
       tho some times we say s/he is dying,
       tho that refers always to something will
       happen in the future.
          We never say s/he dies today,
       a present tense would sound like
       a future, no, dying's always
       in the past,
          always has happened already
       is never more than someone else
       's memory of a past event — as
       if you will never die
       but have always already
       done so in the past.

5/31

To think through a new biology, another
        angle situates hss (homo sap sap):
            world → hu/man ← world

I.E. surrounded by world in & out-
          side:

cells in/of human body total: 30 trillion
        bacteria inside human body
         I.E. human microbiome: 38 trillion

6/2

Woke up with lines from an old poem
        & the image of the kingfisher we
        saw yesterday morning in mind:
            Olson's *Kingfisher* & Mao's quote: La
lumière / de l'aurore / est devant
vous!
          & later: nous devons /
nous lever / et agir.
                From a speech
given December 1947, sets
le la de ce jour,
        the tone of my day, today.

Those 2 3-steps
>   now came back with me thinking
>   not of sunrise, dawn, new be-
>   ginnings & this for me, for my
>   new language, being in the
>   West of my birthlands, in America
>   — the alpha male, the rich, the bitter —
>   but now at 73, of sunset, dusk,
>   a coming darkness, but not
>   mine as much as of
>   that of the new country I had
>   chosen back then, this America,
>   the morning after this
>   bad excuse for a president as much as
>   declares it, the country, under
>   military control.

Has the will to change
>   changed?
>   Or is it only
>   my own old age pulling me
>   down? No dawn
>   left?
>   I did see the
>   kingfisher as black
>   & white,
>   perched
>   on the rusted remains
>   of a 1/2 sunk steel
>   structure in Calvert Vaux
>   Park. It took off
>   who knows whereto — but
>   showed no ill will on no ill wind
>   of change.

6/27

       work ⎱
The poet's walk ⎰   not a line, not
even a or his
          meridian. No: a border/frontier
that is, a territory; a width —

— overheard on radio (France Culture:
          image of poem
as handful of Mikado sticks
dropped on table, needing
to be moved to be read.

*

the idea of purity of language is as ideologically fraught as that of
purity of race, country, nationality.
          The only thing that makes life
possible is the meeting of different elements — they create life (not
some white-bearded old guy)
          The only thing that makes the poem
possible is that same meeting of different elements — a meeting that
creates a tension — a tension that makes sparks fly — sparks that
light up our nights a little bit — or more if we learn how to keep the
sparks flying.

7/16

Predawn Poetics Haiku with German *Einlagen*

The poem, rarely, a *Hauptsatz*.
More often & better, a *Nebensatz*.
At best, however, a *Danebensatz*.

8/13

Paradise is

where land meets sea

where the outside
of our bodies

meets the
inside

9/14

> *On September 14th, Dante's Death Day*

gone for 700 years
>> leaving us here, in the
>> middle kingdom

>> Purgatory
> which was Paradise once
>> but which we soiled

>> and are about to
> turn into hell, or
>> at least an Inferno

for homo sapiens, the
>> disappearing species
>> — if it comes to that —

there's life
>> left, there will be
> life left

>> and right
> it will move
>> on, even without us

it will rejoice in us
gone — I can hear the
birds celebrating

the trees too
the air cooling
the sea cooling

it will be the real paradise
the one sans-sapiens,
that arrogant inter-

ference!

from 11/18

watching
those many
sparrows
bouncing
around
the hedge &
fence takes
a lot of
eyegility.

12/23

the weather holds.
Will I?

UNCOLLECTED POEMS

via Dante, Purgatory

[Lines from Purgatory
(the post-place]

& so it was 800 years ago today, September 14, 2021,
    that Dante Alighieri died in Ravenna, I.E.
        in exile, true dwelling of poets.

Yes, we all know the opening stanza of the Commedia
    "Nel mezzo del cammin di nostra vita
        mi ritrovai per una selva oscura,

ché la diritta via era smarrita." But what interests
    me in Dante's work today are not the power-lusting threats
        for an "Inferno" below for your enemies

or the conmen's promises to the gullible
    for an imaginary "Paradiso" above,
        but the in-between, the barzakh,

in old theological lingo named "Purgatorio"
    — & which is just this here & now
        where we all are & will remain.

Dante's poem of the middle begins :
    Per correr miglior acque alea le vele
        omai la navicella del mio ingegno,

che lascia dietro a sé mar si crudele;
In Allen Mandelbaum's translation:
"To course across more kindly waters now

my talent's little vessel lifts her sails,
leaving behind herself a sea so cruel;
and what I sing will be that second kingdom,

in which the human soul is cleansed of sin,
becoming worthy of ascent to Heaven.
But here, since I am yours, o holy Muses,

may this poem rise again from Hell's dead realm;
and may Calliope rise somewhat here,
accompanying my singing with that music . . ."

from *An AlifBa:* ت T

pour/ for/ für Habib Tengour

Had been looking elsewhere for my
friend, scouring my evolving أبجد
    (oui, je ne suis qu'un *abjadí*) & homer
ed in on *J-*
    -eem but that's too close to home,
as lady N wondered where I was
    wandering off to
        in the distance, I turned my pen around
& spurred it on & into a dream
en français, where
    titubant dans les langues / unsteady in my languages,
      je m'accroche à deux T / I grasp two T's,
Tarafa & Tengour,
        c'était once upon a time
    on boit et chante / we drink & sing
in the *Bar du Soir, (trois amis*
point de mire,
pas d'
exception) archaisms flourish
    Tarafa chantonne in German *du*
Land, wo sonst die Purpurtraube gern
Dem besseren Volke wuchs . . .
you, Habib, interrupt him, saying
    "oh you my شاعر
    Hölderlin gave me an atlal
    a brief pause une pause de courte durée
    with an itinerary
    precise annotations
    I followed"

                    & that's when
I come in pour ajouter mes five
cents or rather my four
                    hundred somethings up or of the air
        for our man Mansur Al-Hallaj
wrote a poem
40 of his Muhatta'at
                with a mim rhyme & a wafer meter
        traces the word
tawhid
through enigmas:
                        "Three letters without
                diacritical signs,
        two with signs and this is
        the whole speech.
        The first points to those
who find it
                & the other serves
        for everyone to say
yes."
        Now apocryphal Tarafa chimes in,
                "as to the other letters,
            it is the mystery of night,
                    no longer a matter
                            of traveling or stopping . . .

(et en rajoute by reciting the atlal
        of his mu'allaqat en anglais:
"Khawla's abandoned campsite :
        an old tattoo's fading glow
            on the schist slopes of Thamad mountain" . . .

We are stopped by & in le *Bar du Soir*
        unstopper the bottles

& travel on, I keep talking, so what's
new, saying
                    "But the only wafer meter I found
        today is a
flow measure, commercially the
Wafer-Style Liquid Flow Meter
                    that shows the curlicues..."
& Tengour éclate de rire & says
        into his glass he takes
                for a microphone:
"handicap of the code . . . des noms insolites . . .
nous ne sommes que lémures / we are but lemurs
échappées des nuits / escaped from the nights
dans le vacarme la soif / in the brouhaha of thirst"
        as I chime in
                or out, "remember my two friends in T
what Shaykh ad-Dabbaagh says about the *ta*
                ﺕ corresponds to the perfection of the apparent
            senses,
                being a part of the Adamic state."
        & united par un profond désir
to stay nomadic here dans la vie
        & there dans les langues
                nous pace up & down les alphabets
no one bets on alpha, the beginning is
        anything, a ruin,
an atlal,
(I keep talking) "anything that starts is already a ruin
        . . . an atlas, no
                an atlal . . . whatever . . .
        that that is the poet's way . . ." mais mes amis
crack up laughing as incapable to pronounce their
language correctly, & made heavy

by drink my tongue
adds another "ta" to atlal,
    turning it into "atlatl" — I too laugh
adding, we are now on that other continent
the one I reached erring (both
meanings at work here) in language &
geography,
   where *atlatl* is a word in
Nahuatl meaning a
     throwing stick for dart or spear
  helps the arm obtain a
thrust of greater velocity
& now Habib s'esclaffe & says "oh,
   un cousin of the kalam, accélère la vitesse de
    la main, je sens le poème qui perce!"
  But it's getting late & some of us
vacillate, though Tarafa's arms
   hold us up,
l'un autour des épaules de Tengour,
  the other around mine,
    as he concludes:
      "Ta is neither here nor there, Ta stands
  for what's complete, remember
'Umar Khayyâm who wrote under
the last poem of the Rubai'yât
Tama'am shud
  it's over, it's done,
    das ist Alles
     Genug!"
& we end or wend there, I say
  ta ta
   & Habib,
     khalâs.

Peace flag,
tattooed no
tattered I
see through
you from land into
sea & nowhere
to land
& vice versa &
versa vice
between between
sun & shade
between light &
water between rock
& land between
wood & rock tattered
flag blood-stained peace
tattooed flag hold
hold hold up
the peace flag
tattooed no tattered
by soldiers washed in
water left not to dry
but to hang
rope & black plastic tatters
hang it all
hangs in no balance
between land & sea a
between you & them

between me & me
along this shore here to reassure me
& you there is blood
slowly washing out
there are holes holes holes
in the flag between
sea & land,
there are algae
adhering to rocks,
waving in the water there is
broken wood waving in
the water.
There are ripped black plastic
bags waving in the wind
calming washing the bloodied flag.

ABOUT THE AUTHOR

Pierre Joris (1946–2025) was a Luxembourger-American poet, essayist, translator, and anthologist who published over eighty books across genres, including more than forty volumes of poetry. *Poasis II: Selected Poems 2000–2024* is the companion volume to *Poasis: Selected Poems 1986–1999* (Wesleyan University Press, 2001).

Joris often referred to his practice as Nomadic Poetics, and wrote extensively about this in essays; his form of writing resists fixed forms, seeking unfamiliar, open structures: not following the conventional idea of "the poem" or the traditional notion of the book.

Also internationally recognized for his translations of Paul Celan, Adonis, Safaa Fathy, Abdelwahab Meddeb, Maurice Blanchot, and others, Joris's translation work was a natural extension of his poetic work—a crossing of languages and sensibilities that deepened the range and resonance of his own writing. In 2020, he received the PEN/Ralph Manheim Medal for Translation and Luxembourg's Batty Weber Lifetime Literary Achievement Prize.

With Jerome Rothenberg he coedited the first two volumes of *Poems for the Millennium*, and coedited the fourth with Habib Tengour. His collaboration with artist-performer Nicole Peyrafitte produced *Domopoetics*, a multimedia fusion of poetry, sound, performance, and visual art that was presented at La Galerie Simoncini in Luxembourg in 2017 and 2021.

Pierre Joris completed the selection for *Poasis II* before his passing on February 26, 2025, in Brooklyn, New York.